ABC Puzzlers

by Ann Richmond Fisher

illustrated by Shelly Rasche

Teaching & Learning Company

1204 Buchanan St., P.O. Box 10
Carthage, IL 62321

This book belongs to

_____

With special thanks to Keith

Cover by Shelly Rasche

Copyright © 1995, Teaching & Learning Company

ISBN No. 1-57310-030-7

Printing No. 987654

Teaching & Learning Company
1204 Buchanan St., P.O. Box 10
Carthage, IL 62321

Table of Contents

Dear Teacher or Parent,

ABC Puzzlers is a book you'll use every day with young students who are learning letters and letter sounds. As they complete pages in this book, students will work on letter recognition and sounds, visual discrimination, matching, noting details and following directions. Students will color, draw, cut and paste as they do a fun variety of activities including puzzles, dot-to-dots, hidden pictures and mazes.

The book contains five pages for each letter of the alphabet. Two of those pages emphasize the shape of the letter as students assemble puzzle pieces, trace the letter or distinguish among similarly shaped letters. The remaining pages for each letter cover the sound of the letter and/or significant objects that begin with that letter. Also, at least one of the five pages gives students practice in cutting with scissors and pasting things together. Answers appear in the back of the book for a few of the trickier puzzles.

This is a functional book that gives your students fun practice in the all-important task of learning their letters. Complete pages can be used for a bulletin board display, to decorate your room for parent conferences, to cover a folder of student work, to send home for review or to include in portfolios of students' work. Your class will enjoy the variety of fun activities, and you will enjoy having such a useful book at your fingertips!

Sincerely,

Ann

Ann Richmond Fisher

Color all the spaces with A inside.

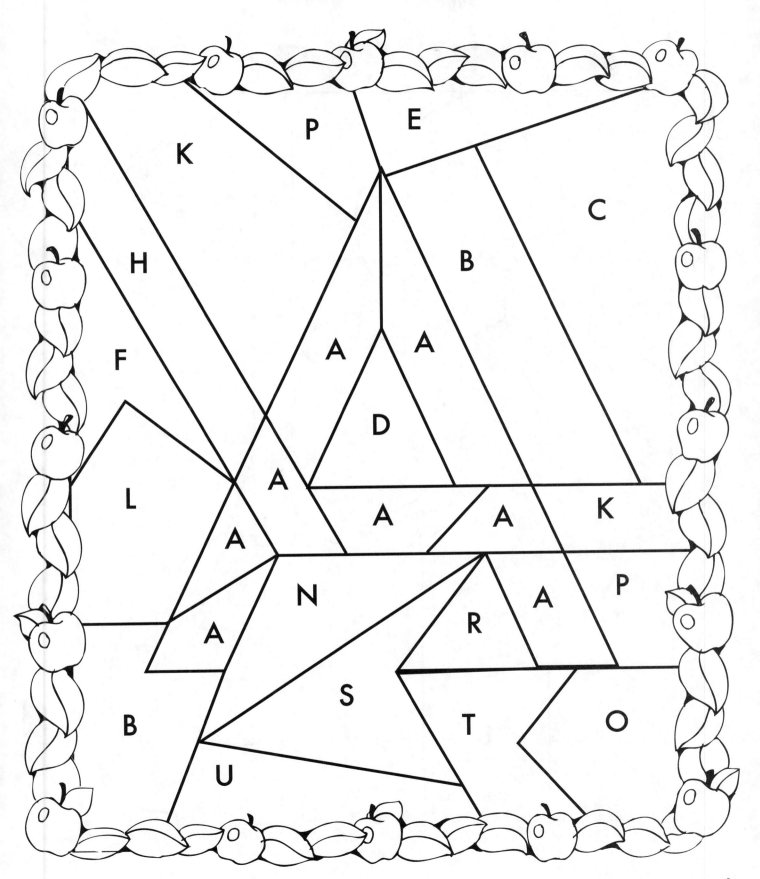

1

Aa

Color all the spaces with **a** inside.

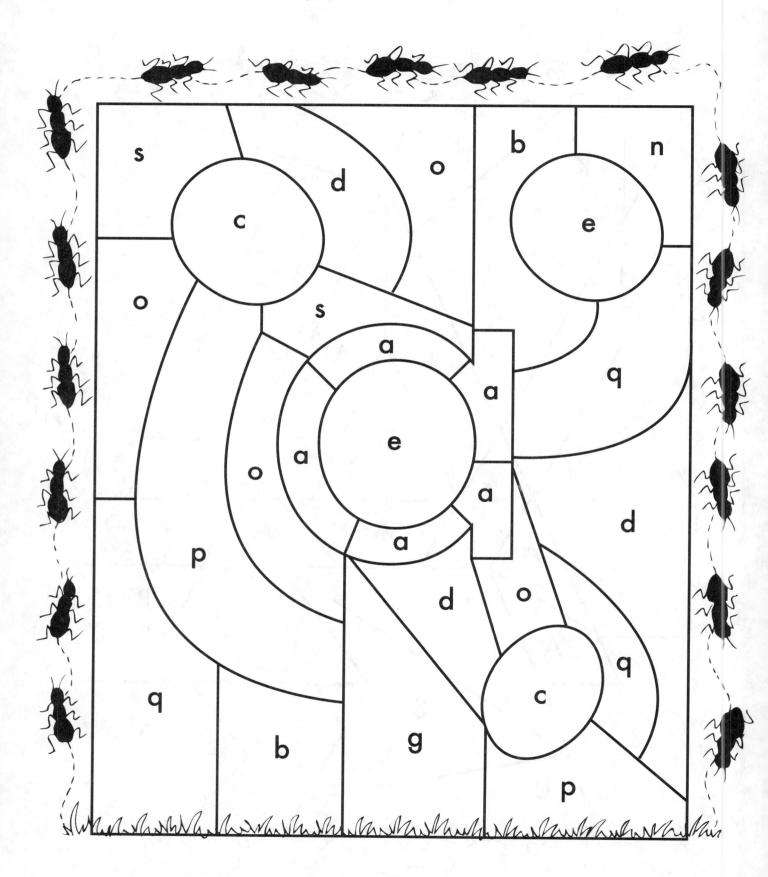

2

A is for *apple.*

Color the apples red.   Color the tree green and brown.

Cut out the apples.   Paste them on the tree.

Aa

Aa

A is for *abacus.*
Color the beads in each row to match the number.

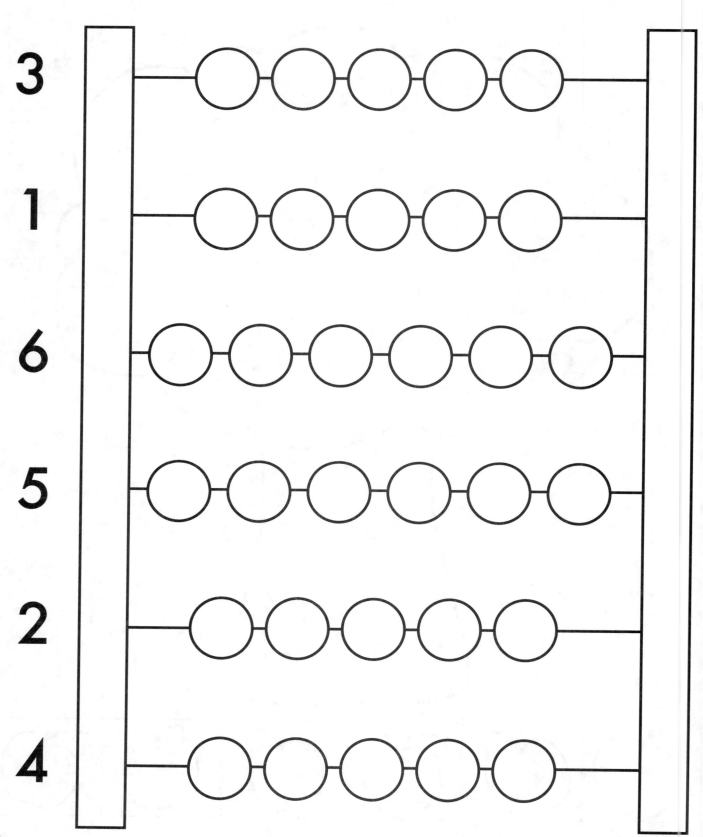

3

1

6

5

2

4

Color the pictures that begin with the long **a** sound as in *acorn.* Circle the pictures that begin with the short **a** sound as in *apple.*

ape	ant	apron
ax	anchor	alligator
angel	astronaut	antlers

Bb

Color the puzzle pieces.
Cut out the pieces. Paste them on paper to make a **B**.

6

Color the puzzle pieces.
Cut out the pieces. Paste them on paper to make a **b**.

Bb

Bb

B is for *button.*
Draw lines to connect the buttons that are the same.
Color the pairs of buttons to match.

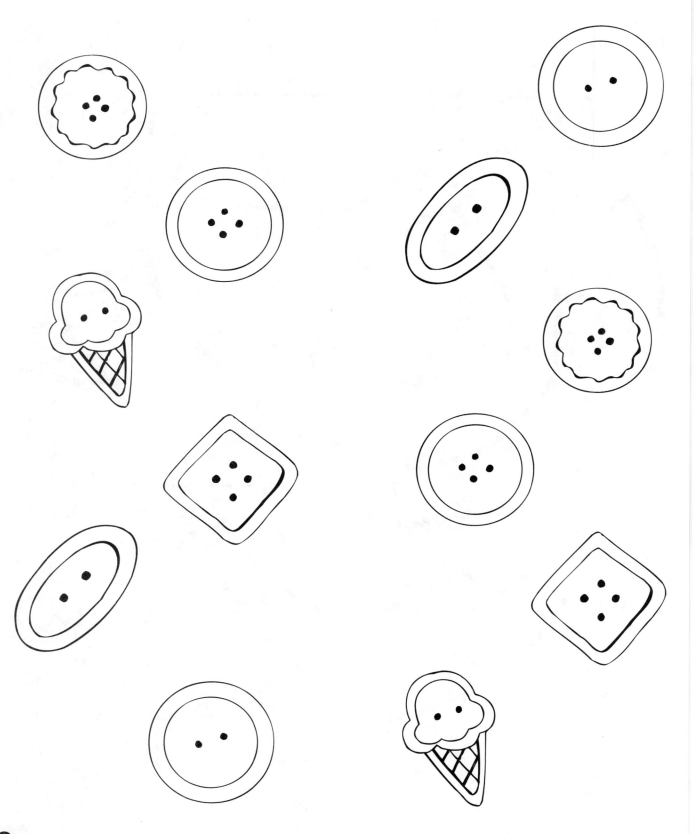

8

Color the **B** things that are alive.

baby	bell	butterfly
ball	bear	book
bird	boy	balloon

Bb

B is for *book*. Color these pages and cut them out. Fold the pages on the dotted line. Put them together and staple them to make a book. Draw more **b** pictures on the blank pages.

box

butterfly

Trace and color.

Cc

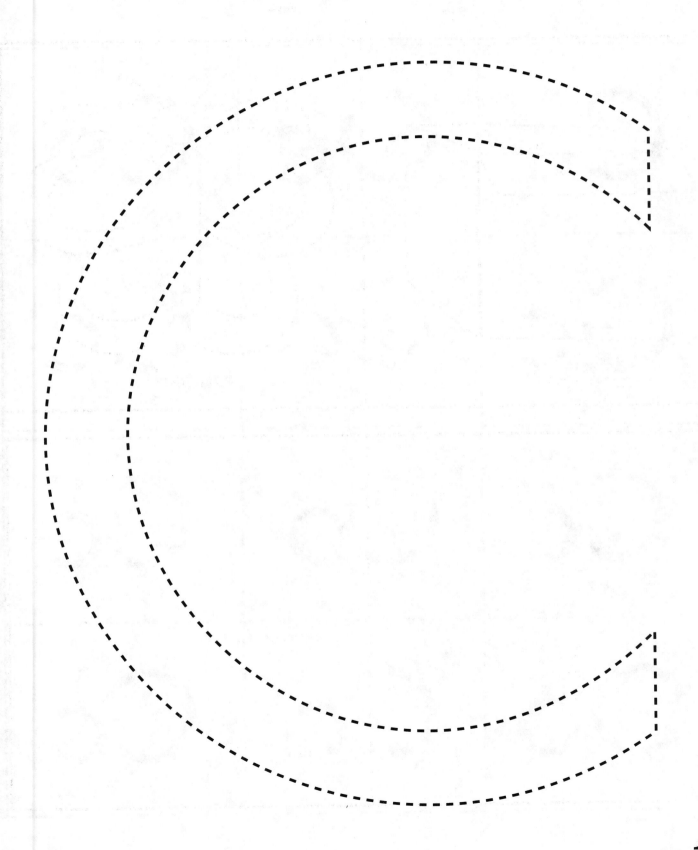

Cc

Cut out the letter boxes.
Paste only the boxes with two **C**s on your paper.
Draw a picture of a word that starts with **C.**

Cc	Oc	Ce
Gc	Cc	Cc
Cc	Co	Cc
Oo	Cc	Cc

12

C is for *circles.*

How many circles do you see?

_____

How many circles do you see?

_____

Cc

Circle the **C** words that start with the **s** sound.
Underline the **C** words that start with the **k** sound.
Color all the pictures.

cent	cat	cake
coat	celery	city
candy	centipede	cup

14

C is for *clown, cap, collar* and *color*. First draw a funny face on the clown. Then add a cap and a collar. Last, color the clown.

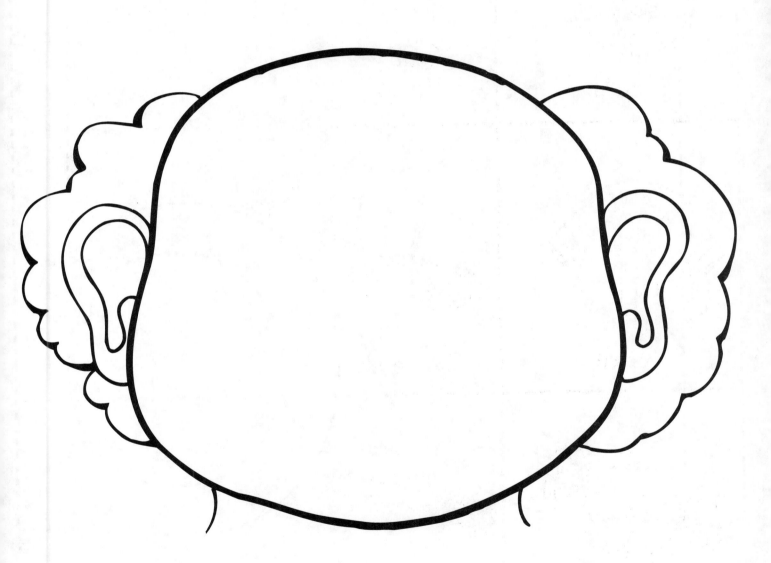

Dd

Trace and color.

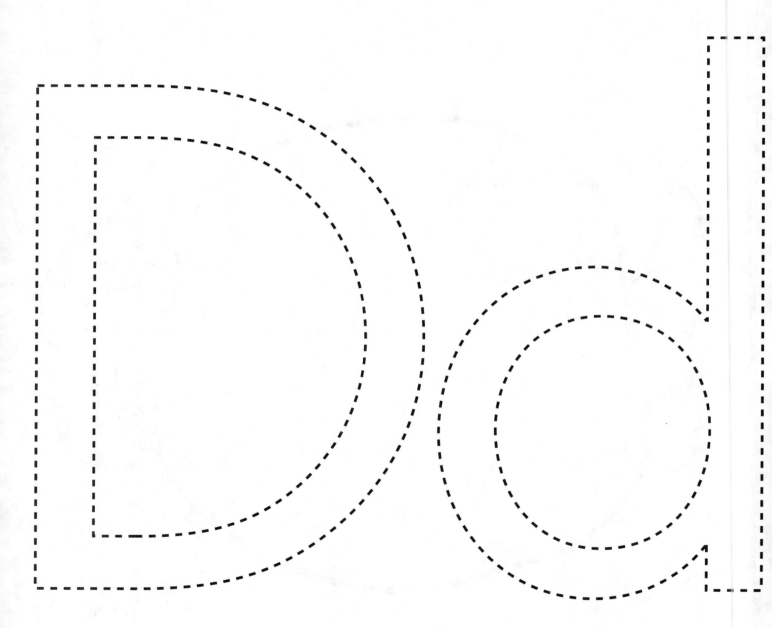

16

Cut out the letter boxes.
Paste only the boxes with two Ds on your paper.
Draw a picture of a word that starts with D.

Db	Dd	Dd
Bd	Dd	Dp
Dd	Rd	Dd
Db	Dd	Db

Dd

D is for *dominoes.*
Cut out the dominoes. Match the ends and paste them on your paper.

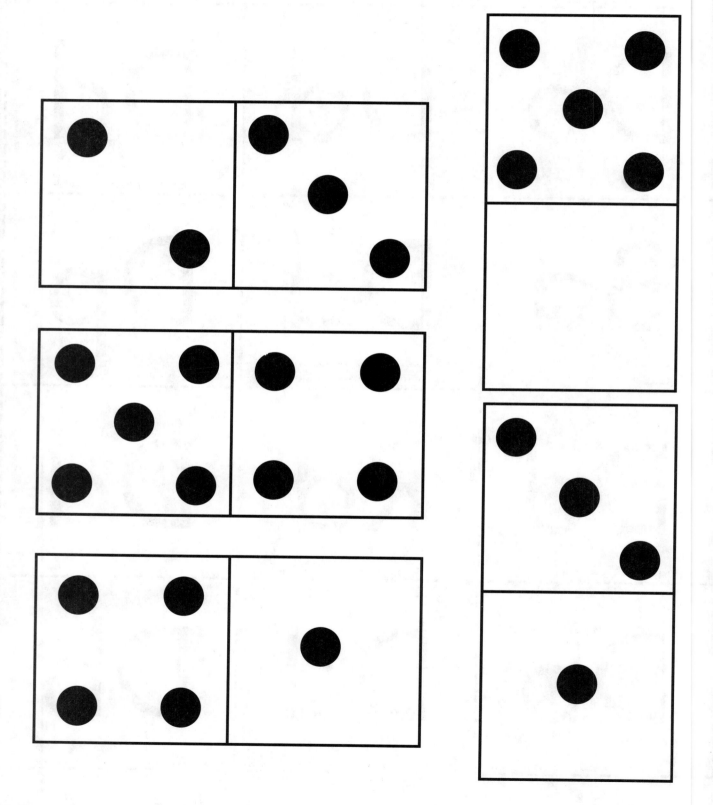

18

Color the toys that start with **D**.

Dd

D is for *diamond*. This shape is a diamond:
Color all the diamonds red.
Color the other shapes blue.

Connect the dots. Start with 1.
Color the shape you make.

1

17

2

3

5

4

16

6

7

9

8

15

10

11

14

13

12

Ee

T race and color.

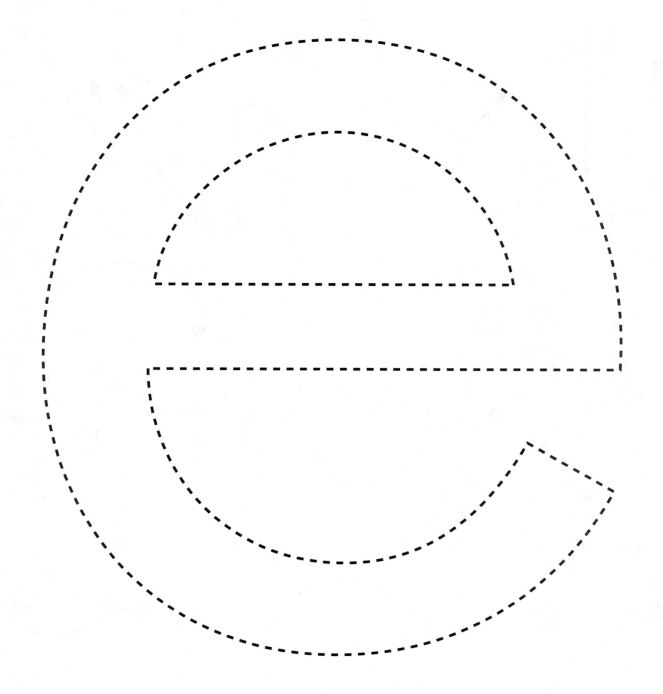

E is for *egg*. Cut out the eggshells. Match the halves.
Paste them together on your paper. Color the eggs.

Ee

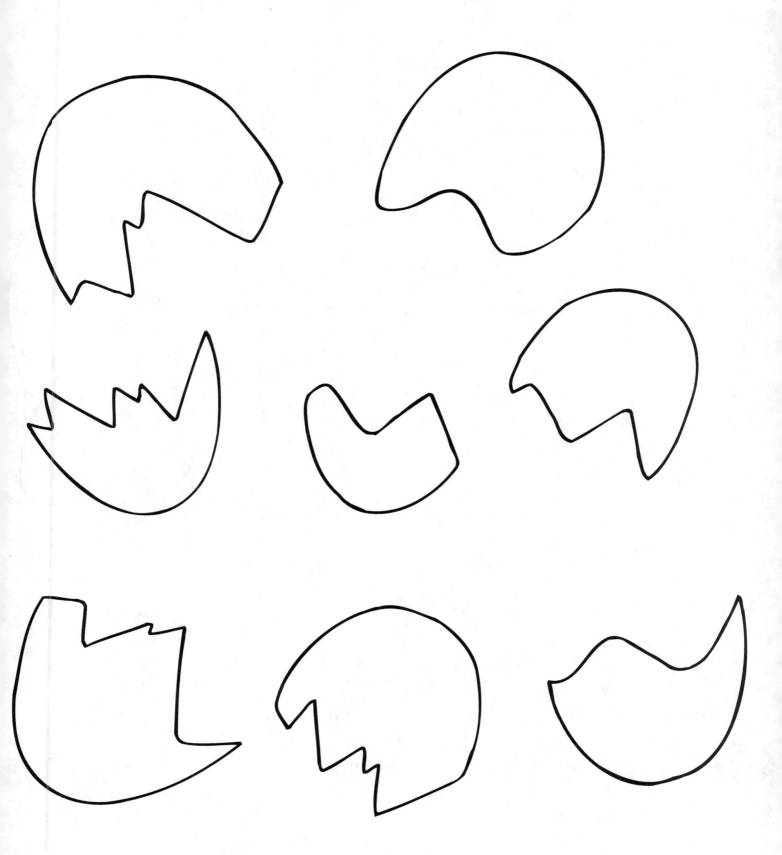

Ee

E is for *elephant.* Draw lines from the peanuts to the elephants so each elephant gets the same number of peanuts. Color the picture.

24

Color the words that begin with the long **e** sound as in *eel*.
Circle the words that begin with the short **e** sound as in *egg*.

Ee

| Eskimo | envelope | easel |
| elevator | Easter basket | elf |

25

Ff

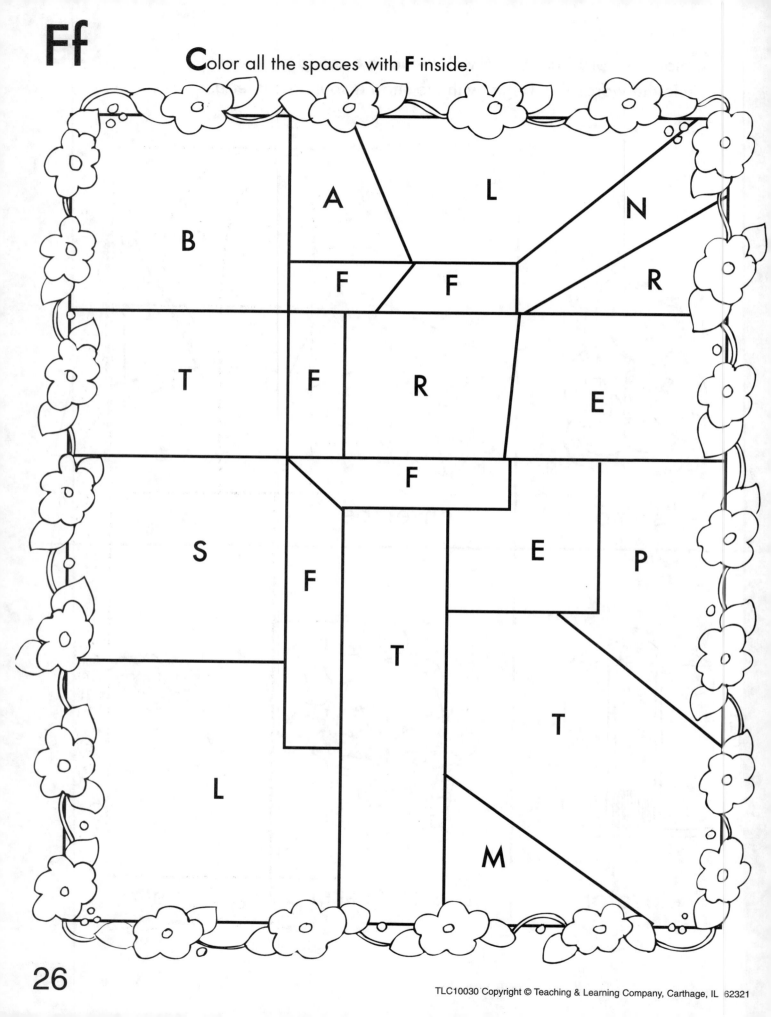

A L N

B

F F R

T F R E

F

S E P

F

T T

L M

26

Ff

Color all the spaces with **f** inside.

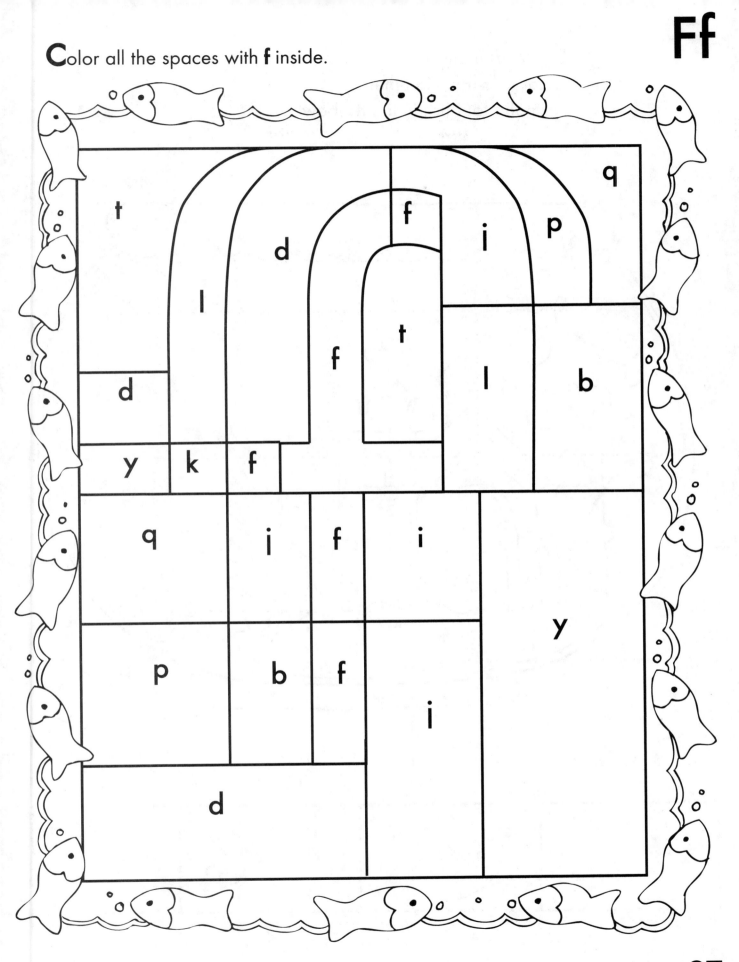

27

Ff

F is for *fish* and *four*.
Color four fish. Cut them out.
Paste the four fish in the fishbowl.

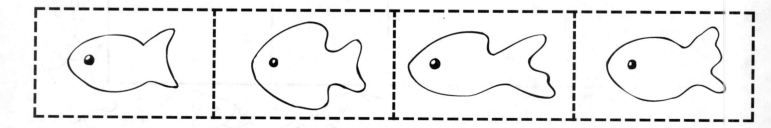

28

F is for *farm.* Circle the things in the bottom farm that are different from the farm on the top.

Ff

Ff

F is for *faucet* and *full*. Color the faucet gray.
Draw blue water coming out of the faucet to make the jar *full*.

30

Color the puzzle pieces. Cut them out.
Paste the pieces on paper to make a **G**.

Gg

Gg

Color the puzzle pieces. Cut them out.
Paste the pieces on paper to make a **g**.

32

G is for *globe.* Color the globe by matching the numbers with the colors.

1 = green   2 = blue   3 = brown

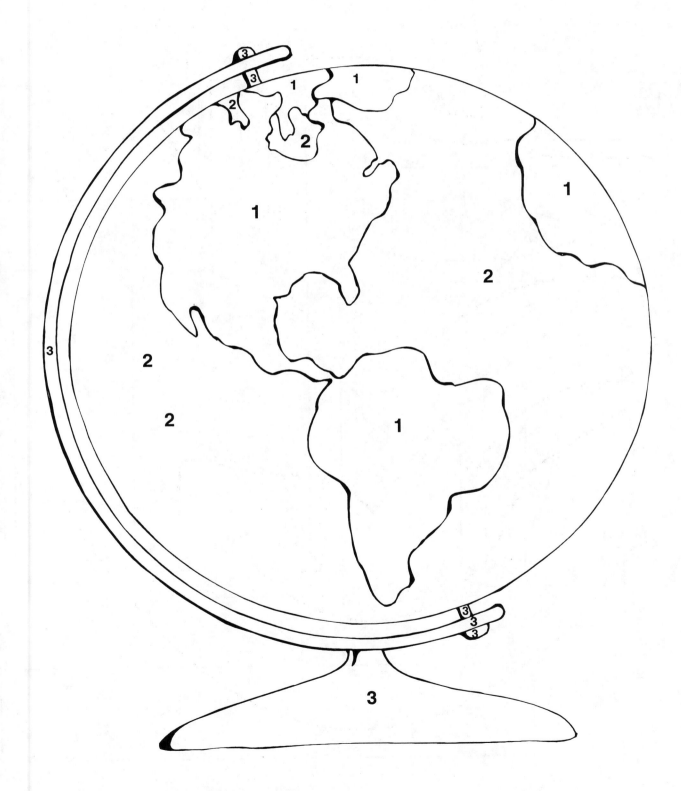

Gg

Cut out the pieces.
Put them together to make three animals that start with **G**.
(You need three pieces for each animal.)
Color the animals. Paste them on your paper.

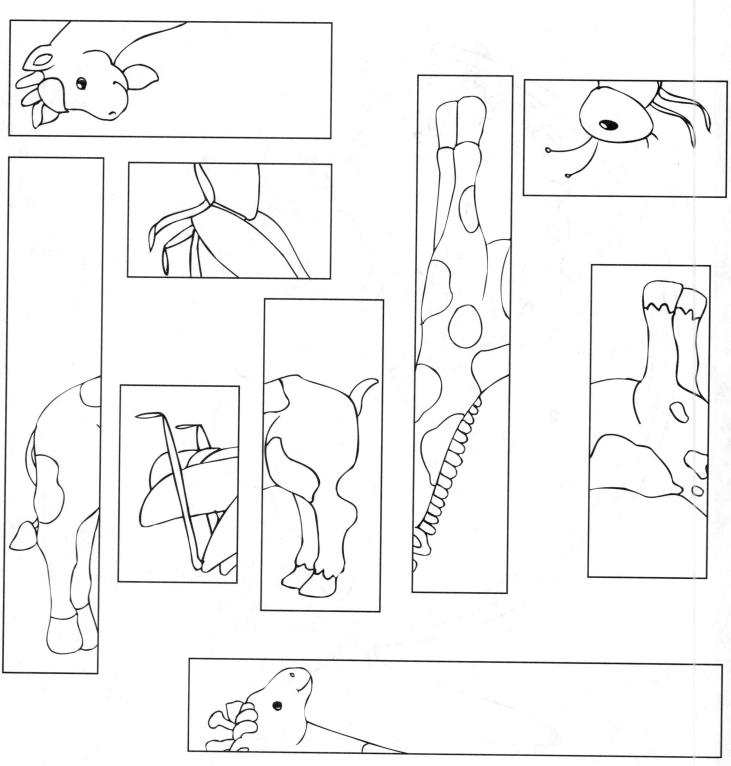

34

G is for *grapes.* Color the grapes in the big bunch green.
Color the grapes in the little bunch purple.

Gg

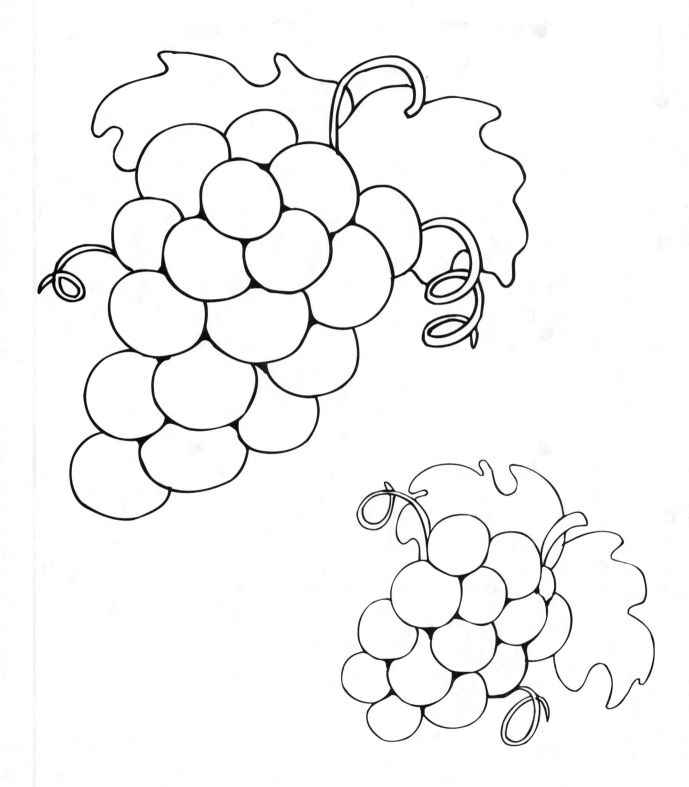

Connect the dots. Start with letter A.
Color the shape you make.

A ●   ● B   E ●   ● F

Q ●

P ●

C ●   D ●   ● G

L ●   K ●

O ○ ●

H ●

N ●   ● M   J ●   ● I

 Trace and color.

 Hh

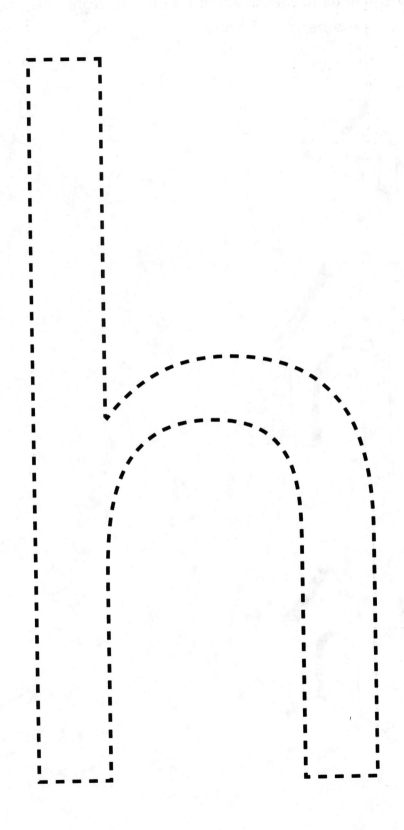

Hh

H is for *hens* and *houses*.
Draw lines to match each hen to the right-sized henhouse.
Color the hens and houses.

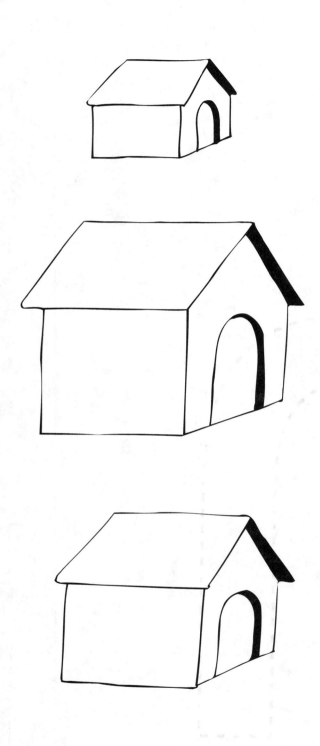

H is for *hat*. Color the people and the hats.
Cut out the hats and paste them on the right person.

Hh

H is for *heavy*.
Color the object in each box that is heavy.

40

Trace and color.

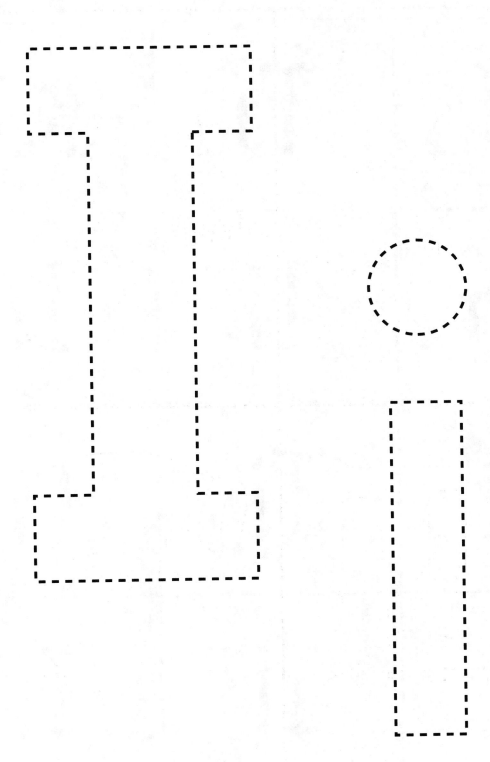

Ii

Cut out the letter boxes.
Paste only the boxes with two **I**s on your paper.
Draw a picture of a word that starts with **I**.

Ii	Ti	Ki
In	Ii	Ii
Tt	Ii	Li
Ii	Il	Ii

I is for *ice skating.*

Color the two ice skaters that are dressed the same.

Ii

Ii

I is for *igloo*.
Color each igloo you find in the hidden picture.

Color the pictures that begin with the long **i** sound as in *ice*.
Circle the pictures that begin with the short **i** sound as in *igloo*.

insect

icicle

island

iron

inchworm

iris

Jj

Color all the spaces with **J** inside.

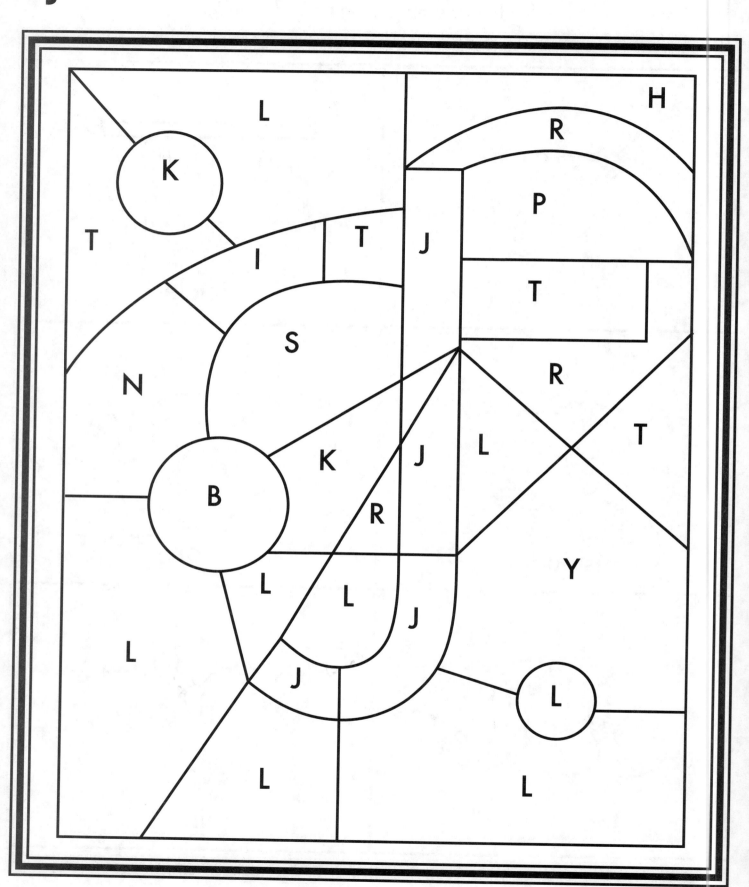

Color all the spaces with **j** inside.

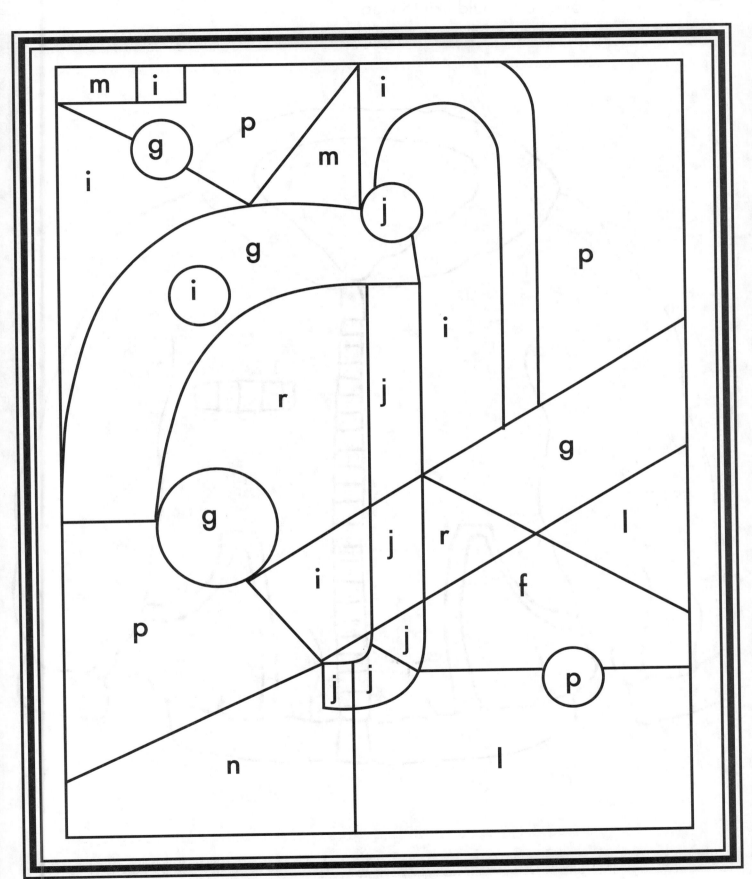

Jj

J is for *jacket*. Color this jacket so it looks like one you would like to wear.

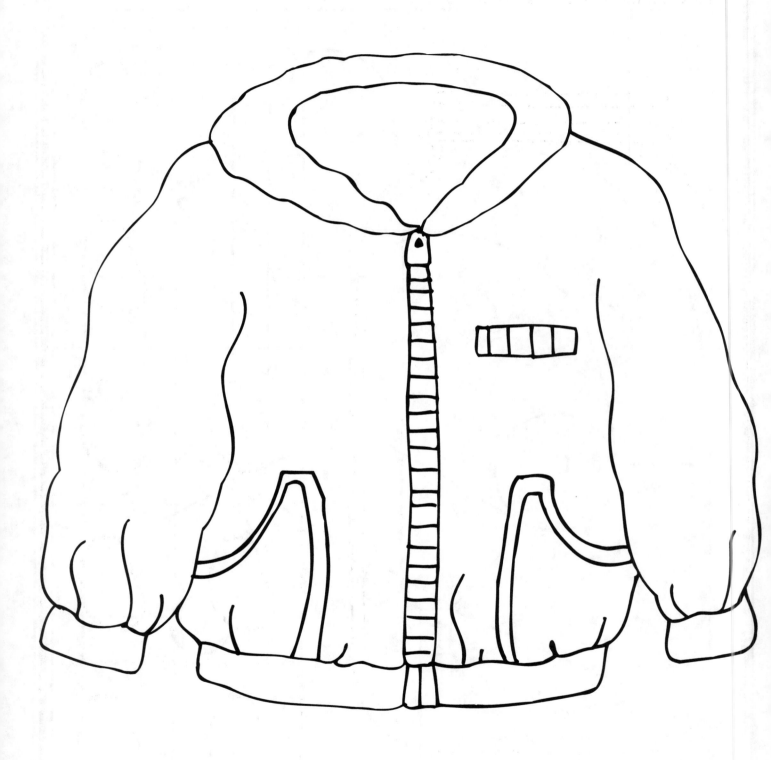

48

J is for *jelly beans.* Color three jelly beans red.
Color two jelly beans green. Color four jelly beans orange.
Cut out all the jelly beans and paste them in the jar.
How many jelly beans are there in all?

Jj

J is for *jeep*.
Add lines to the bottom picture to make it match the top picture.

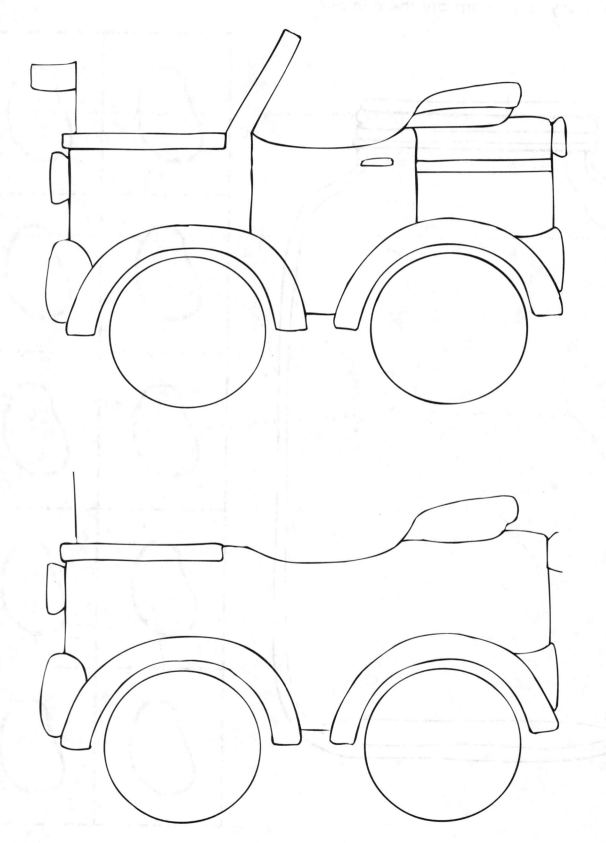

Color the puzzle pieces. Cut out the pieces.
Paste them on paper to make a **K**.

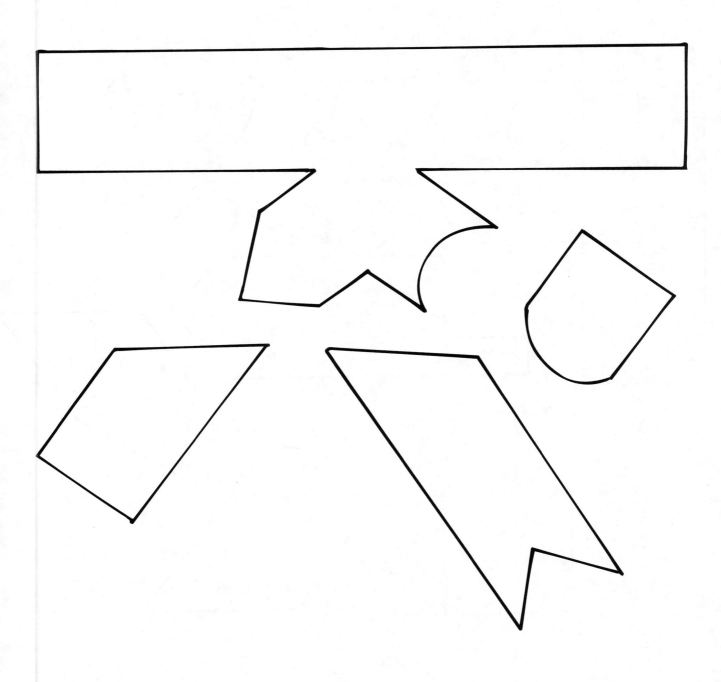

Kk

Color the puzzle pieces. Cut out the pieces.
Paste them on paper to make a **k**.

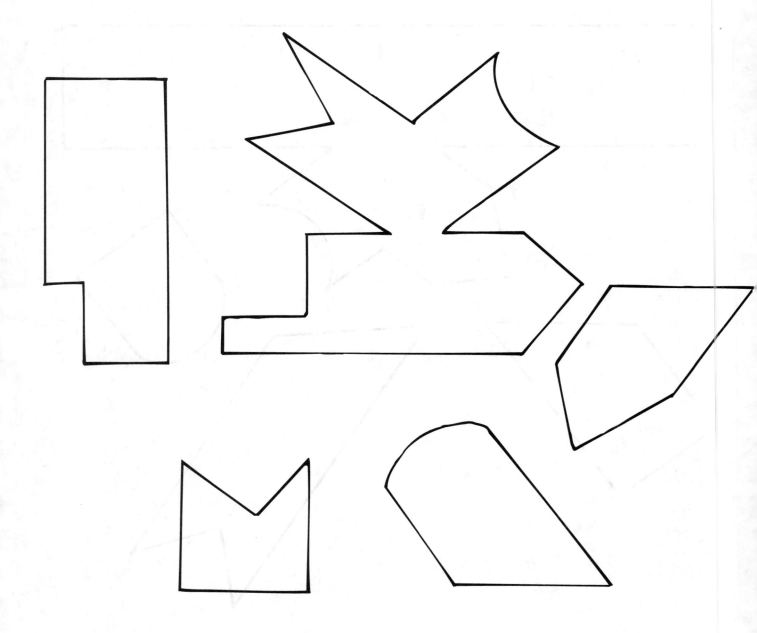

K is for *kite*. Find which kite belongs to each person.
Color one boy's kite green.   Color the girl's kite red.
Color the other boy's kite yellow.

Kk

K is for *keys*. Draw a line from each key on the left to a matching key on the right.

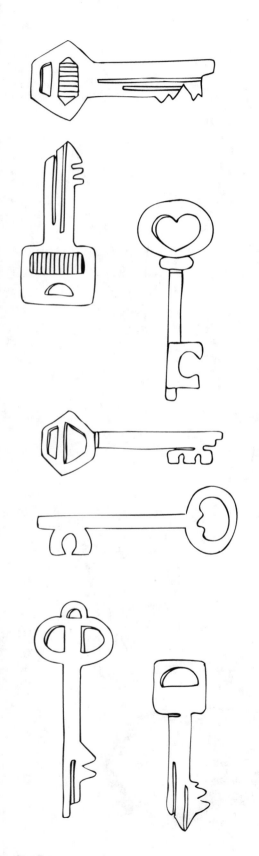

K is for *kangaroo*. Color both kangaroos. Cut them out. Put the baby kangaroo in the mother's pouch. Paste them both on another sheet of paper.

L l

Connect the dots. Start with letter **a**.
Color the shape you make.

k

j ●   ●━━━● a

i ●   ● b

h ●   ● c

g ●   ● d

f ●   ● e

Connect the dots. Start with number 1.
Color the shape you make.

12 ●   **13**
●━━━━━● 1

11 ●   ● 2

10 ●   ● 3

       4   5
      ●   ●   ● 6

9 ●   ●   ● 7
       8

L l

L is for *light*.
Color the things that give light.

L is for *lane, limousine* and *left*. Color the limousine.
Cut it out. Paste it in the left lane.

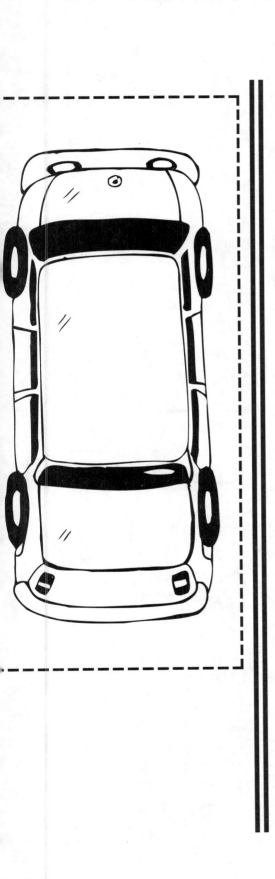

L l

L is for *lollipop.*

Match the numbers to the colors to color each lollipop.

1 = yellow   2 = pink   3 = orange   4 = green

Color all the spaces with **M** inside.

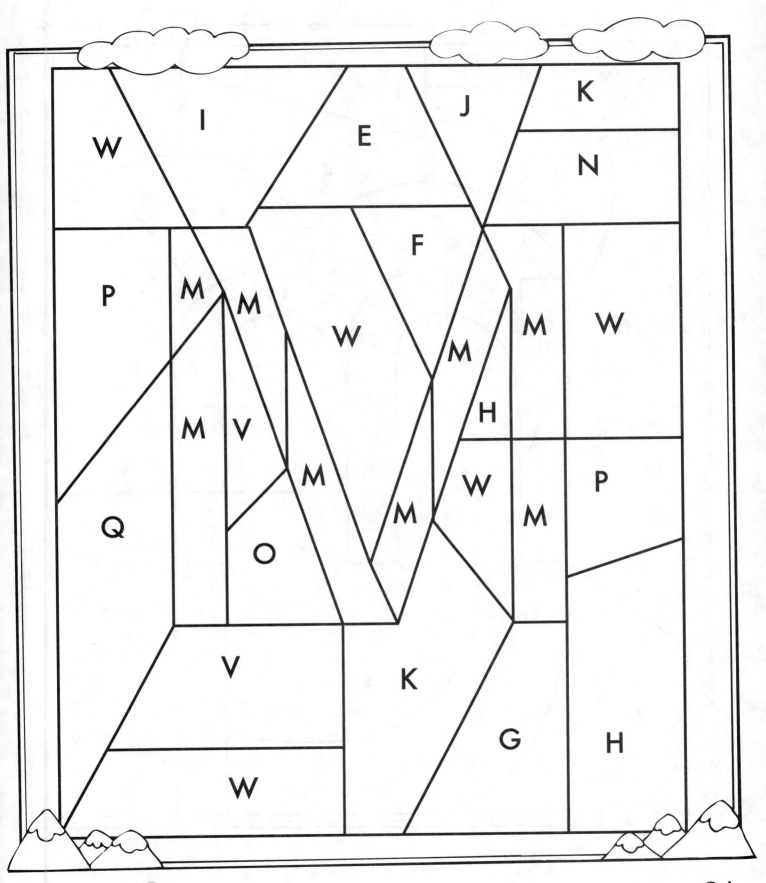

TLC10030 Copyright © Teaching & Learning Company, Carthage, IL 62321

Mm

Color all the spaces with **m** inside.

w

n

o

x

c

s

r

w

m

m

w

m

w

w

n

m

m

r

m

s

n

s

w

p

o

M is for *megaphone*. Color the cheerleaders and megaphones. Cut out the megaphones. Paste each one in the hands of the cheerleader with the same letter.

Mm

M is for *mountain* and *maze*. Draw a path through the maze.

M is for *monkeys* and *most*.
Color all the monkeys.
Circle the monkey with the *most* bananas.

Nn

Trace and color.

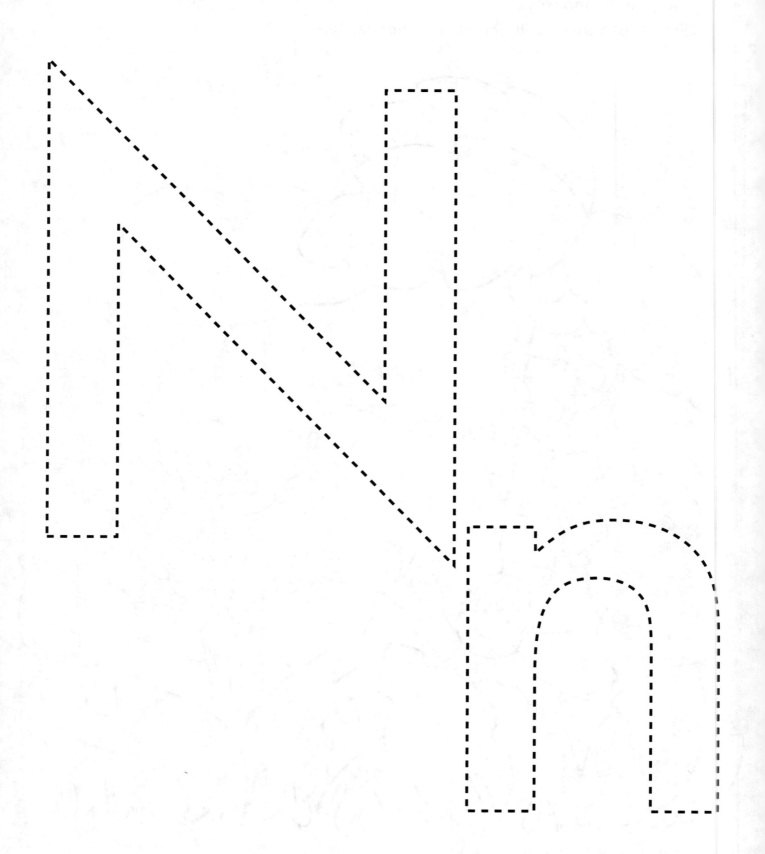

Cut out the letter boxes.
Paste only the boxes with two **N**s on your paper.
Draw a picture of a word that starts with **N**.

Nn	Nm	Mn
Nr	Nn	Wn
Nn	Mm	Nn
Vn	Nn	Nn

Nn

N is for *nose*. Draw a nose on each face.
Color the pictures.

N is for *numbers*. Circle the numbers.
Put an **X** on the letters.

B

C

1

2

D

3

H

5

K

3

4

F

P

5

2

8

S

7

M

6

N

3

9

7

10

I

A

9

L

R

E

J

G

8

Q

Nn

N is for *next*. Write the letter that comes next in the alphabet beside each letter below.

A _____	E _____
F _____	J _____
M _____	B _____
I _____	G _____
C _____	N _____
H _____	K _____
L _____	D _____

Trace and color.

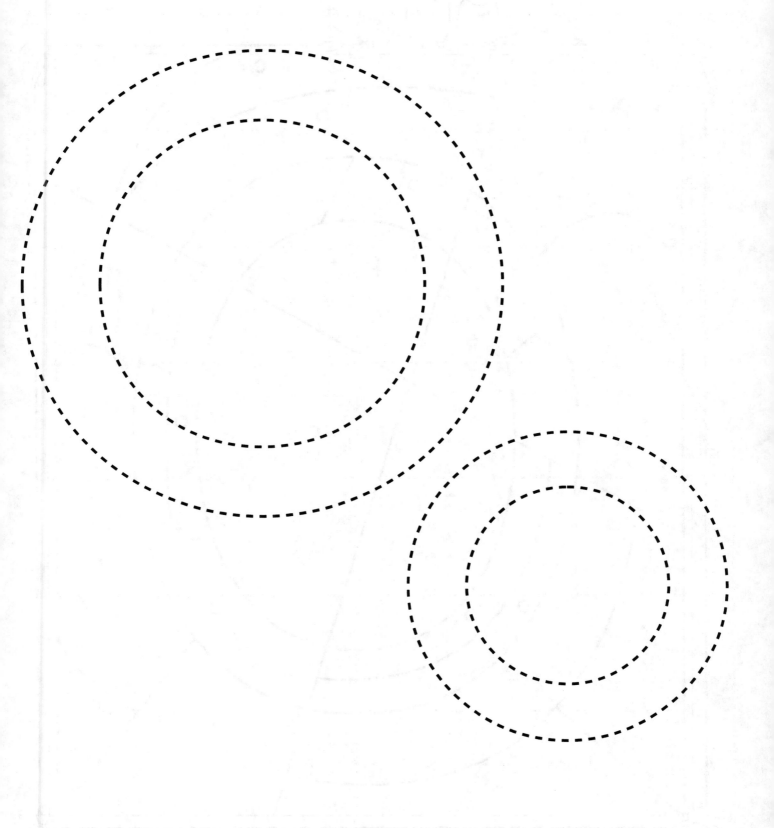

Oo

Color all the spaces with o inside.

a

c

d

a

o

o

o

p

q

c

e

o

o

c

a

o

o

c

a

o

o

o

c

a

e

r

O is for *oval*.

How many ovals do you see? _____

How many ovals do you see? _____

Oo

O is for *ostrich* and *owl*. Color both animals.
Cut out the animals. Paste the owl in the tree.
Paste the ostrich on the ground.

74

Color the pictures that begin with the long **o** sound as in *open*. Circle the pictures that begin with the short **o** sound as in *on*.

oval

olive

octopus

oboe

otter

oatmeal

Pp

Cut out the letter boxes.
Paste only the boxes with two **P**s on your paper.
Draw a picture of a word that starts with **P** on your paper.

Pp	Bp	Pp
Pq	Pp	Pp
Pp	Pg	Dp
Po	Pp	Pp

Color the puzzle pieces. Cut out the pieces.
Paste them on your paper to make a **P**.

Pp

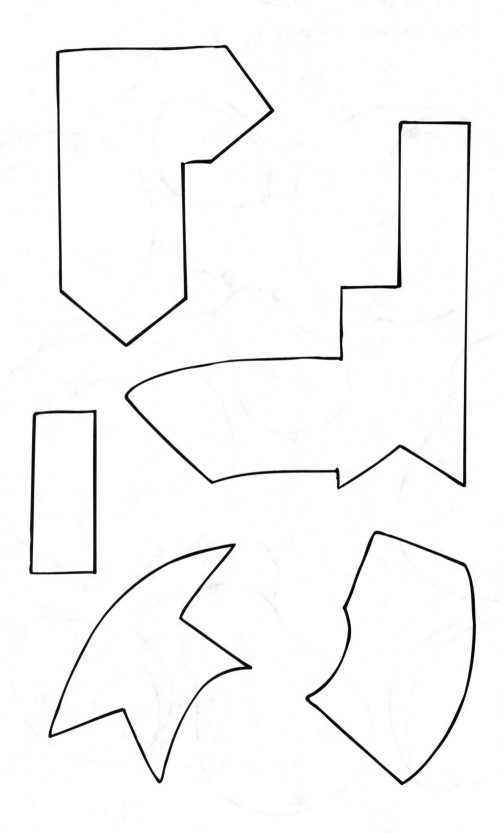

77

Pp

P is for *peaches, pears* and *plums.*

Color the peaches ⬭ orange.

Color the pears 🍐 yellow.

Color the plums ⬭ purple.

P is for *pairs*. Draw lines to match the pairs of socks.
Color the socks.

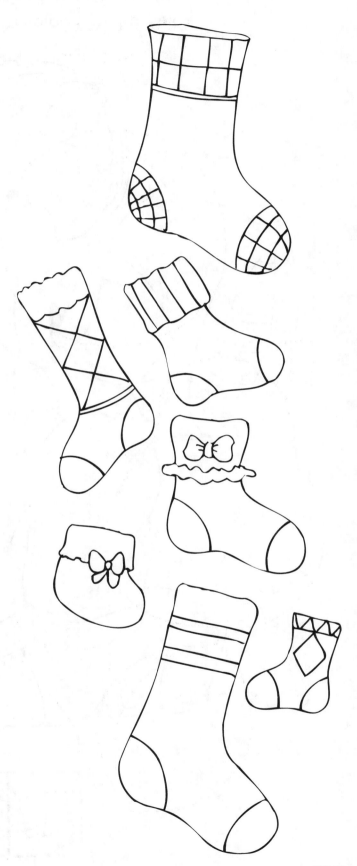

Pp

P is for *Paul, pajamas, patch* and *paste*. Color Paul in his paja-mas. Color the patches. Cut them out and paste them on the holes in Paul's pajamas.

80

Cut out the letter boxes.
Paste only the boxes with two **Q**s on your paper.
Draw a picture of a word that starts with **Q** on your paper.

Oq	Qq	Qg
Qq	Oq	Qq
Qp	Qq	Qq
Qq	Qq	Qo

81

TLC10030 Copyright © Teaching & Learning Company, Carthage, IL 62321

Qq

Trace and color.

82

Q is for *quarter*. Color the quarters gray.
Cut them out and paste them in the piggy bank.

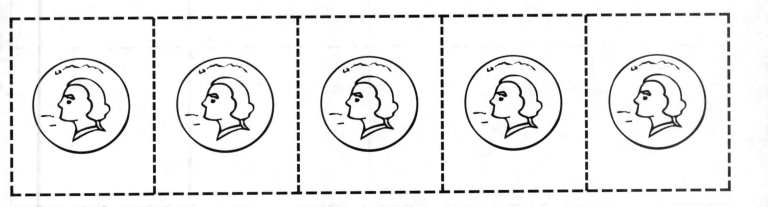

Qq

Q is for *quilt*.

Color the squares in the quilt to make a pattern.

Q is for *quartet* and *quail*. Here is a quartet of quails.
Circle the quail that is different from the other three.
Color all the quails.

Rr

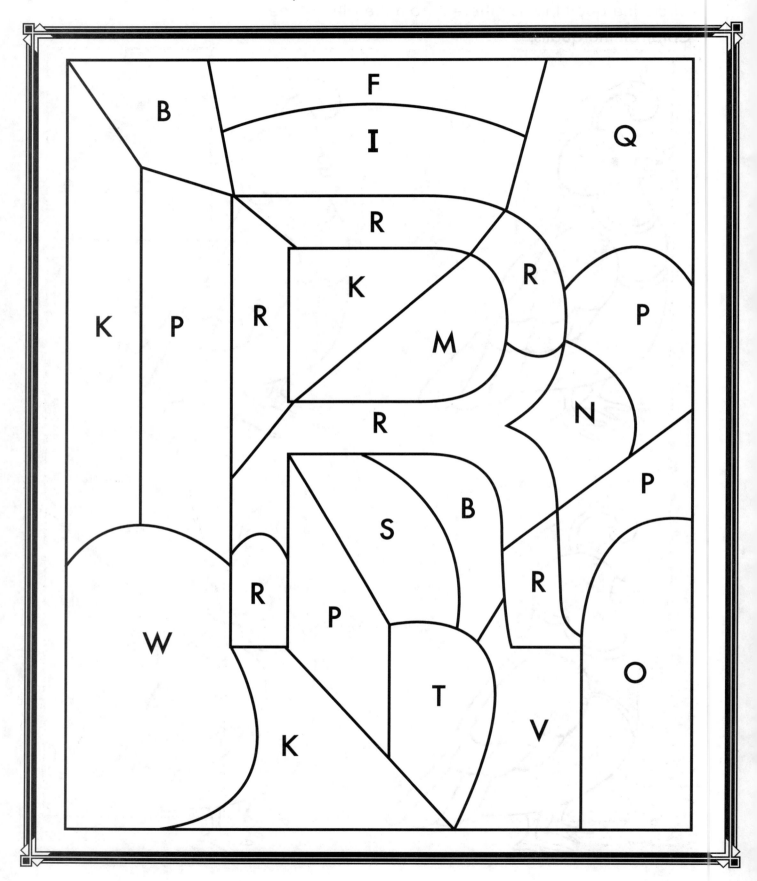

Color all the spaces with **r** inside.

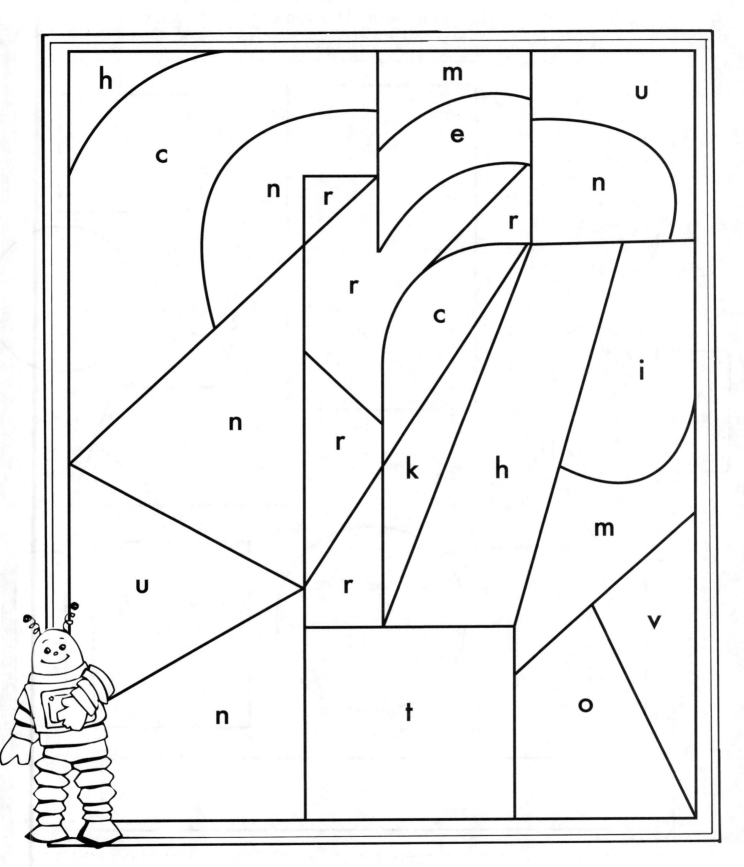

Rr

R is for *robot*. Cut out these parts. Paste them on your paper to create your own robot. Draw in a face and other parts.

R is for *reptile*. Reptiles are animals covered with scales or hard plates. Turtles and snakes are reptiles. Color all the reptiles below.

Rr

snake

bear

turtle

dog

ape

alligator

Rr

R is for *red* and *ruler.* Color the ruler red. Cut it out. Find something in your room that is 6 inches (15 cm) long.

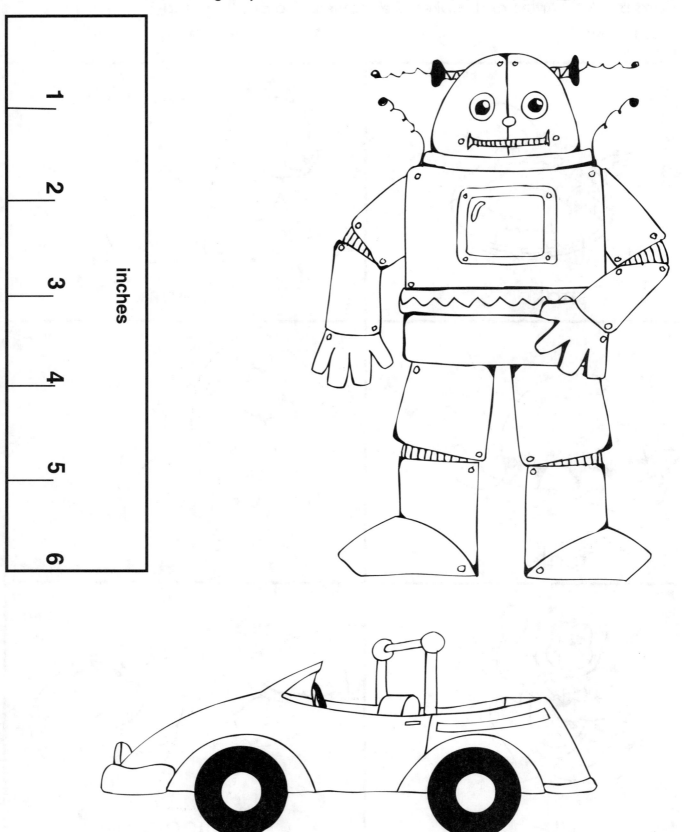

inches

1
2
3
4
5
6

Color the puzzle pieces. Cut out the pieces.
Paste them on paper to make an **S**.

Ss Trace and color.

92

Ss

Color only the animals that start with **s**.

seal	tiger	snake
skunk	sheep	lion
horse	snail	spider

Ss

S is for *seashore, sea horse, seashell, starfish* and *sunshine*.
Circle all the things that are different in the bottom picture.

94

S is for *scale* and *six*. Color the scale. Color the six balls. Cut them out and paste them on both sides of the scale so it will balance.

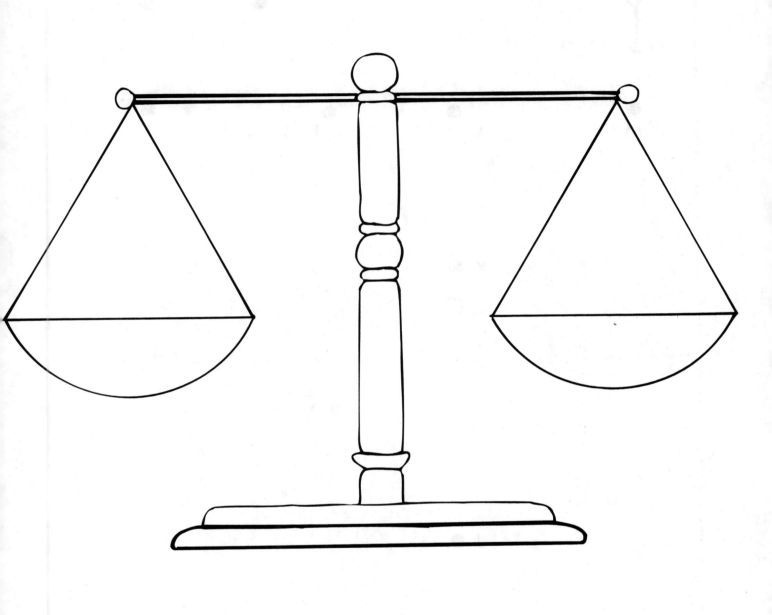

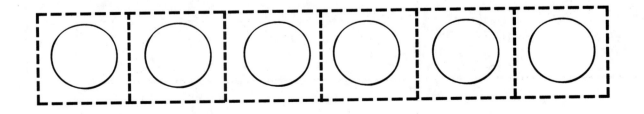

Tt

Connect the dots. Start with letter **A**.
Color the shape you make.

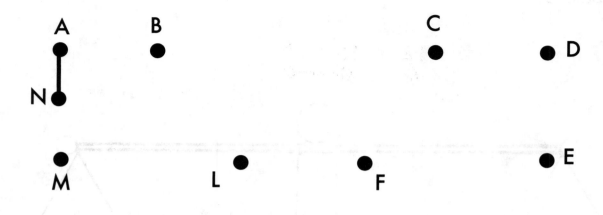

A
B
C
D
N
M
L
F
E
K
G
J
I
H

96

Connect the dots. Start with number 1.
Color the shape you make.

14   15   1

13   2   3

12   2   3

11   4

10   5

9

6

8   7

Tt

T is for *tools*. Color the tools. Cut them out.
Paste them on paper in order from smallest to largest.
Put the smallest tool at the top of your paper and the largest
at the bottom.

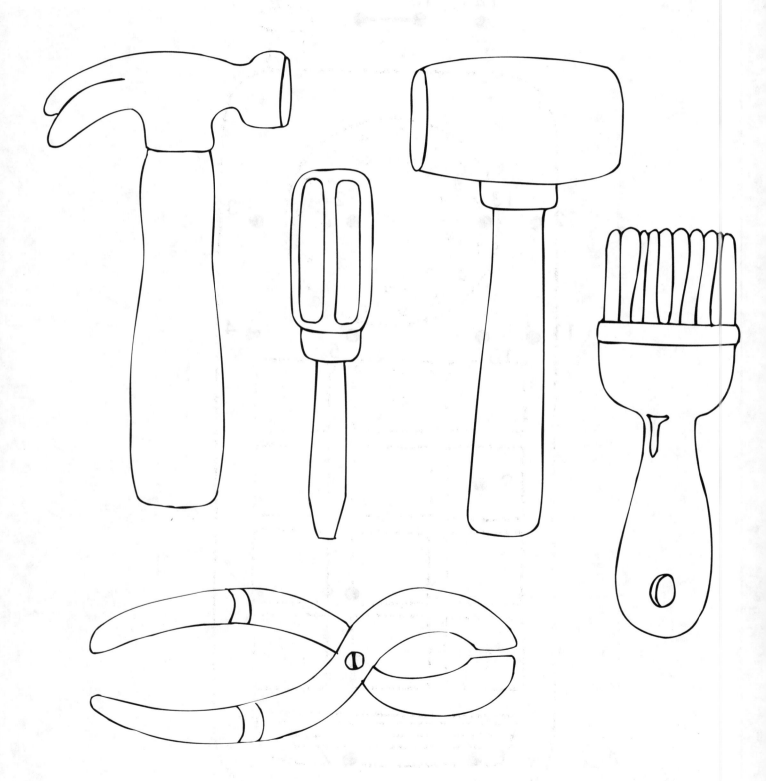

98

T is for *telephone*.
Write the numbers 0-9 on the correct buttons on the tele-phone.

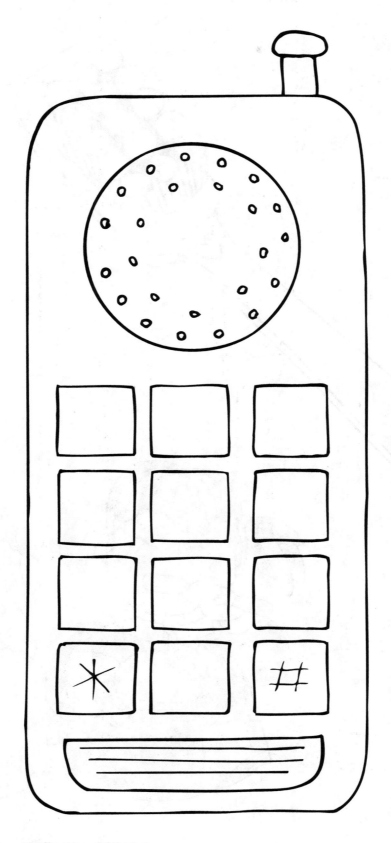

Tt

T is for *toothbrush*. Color this toothbrush to match the one you use at home. Draw your favorite kind of toothpaste on the toothbrush. How many times a day do you brush your teeth? _____

Trace and color.

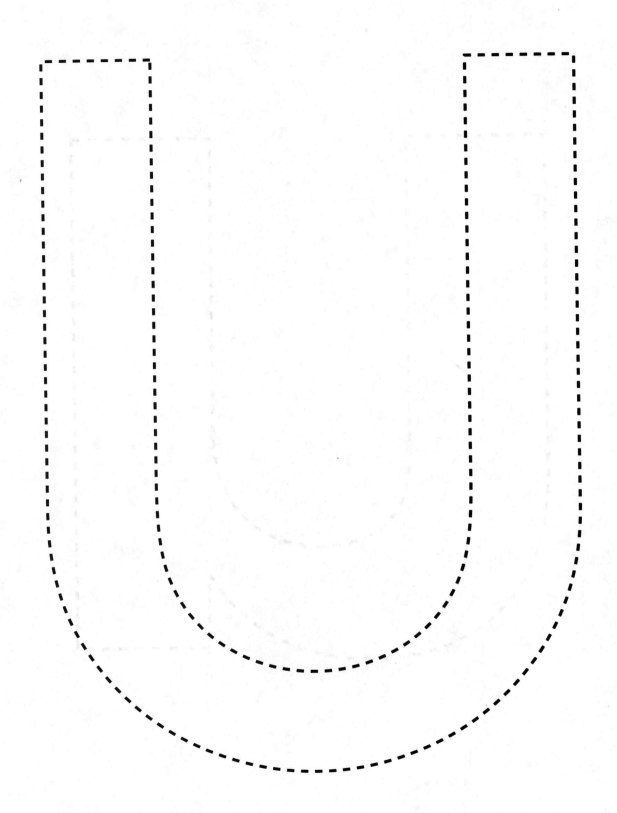

Uu

Trace and color.

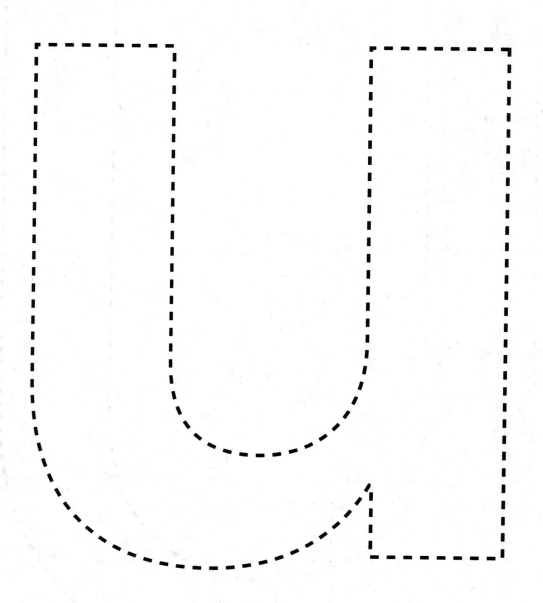

U is for *uniform*. Color the fire fighter and police officer's uniforms. Cut out the uniforms and paste on the fire fighter and police officer.

Uu

U is for *umbrella*. Color each umbrella you find in the hidden picture.

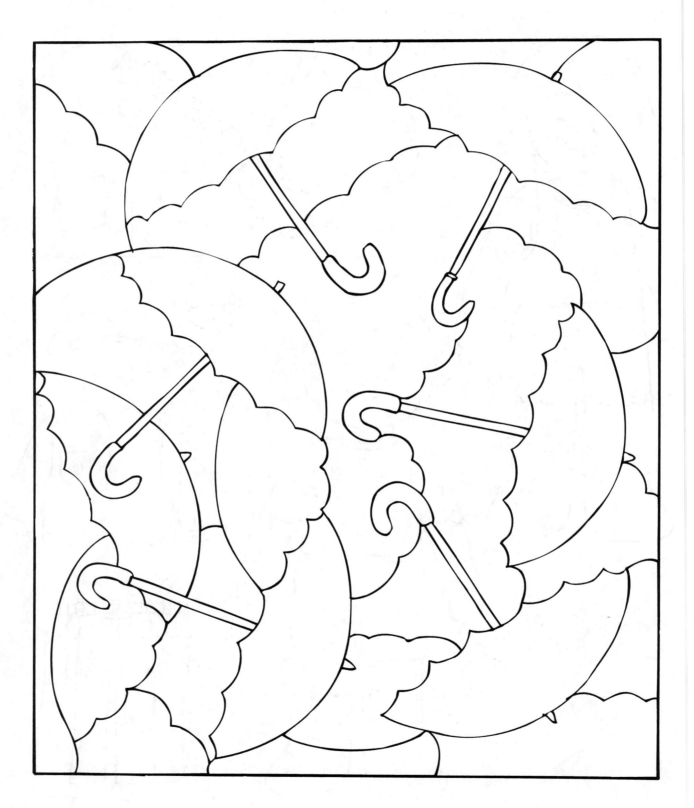

104

Color the words that have the long **u** sound as in *use*.
Circle the pictures that have the short **u** sound as in *under*.

Vv

Connect the dots. Start with **a**.

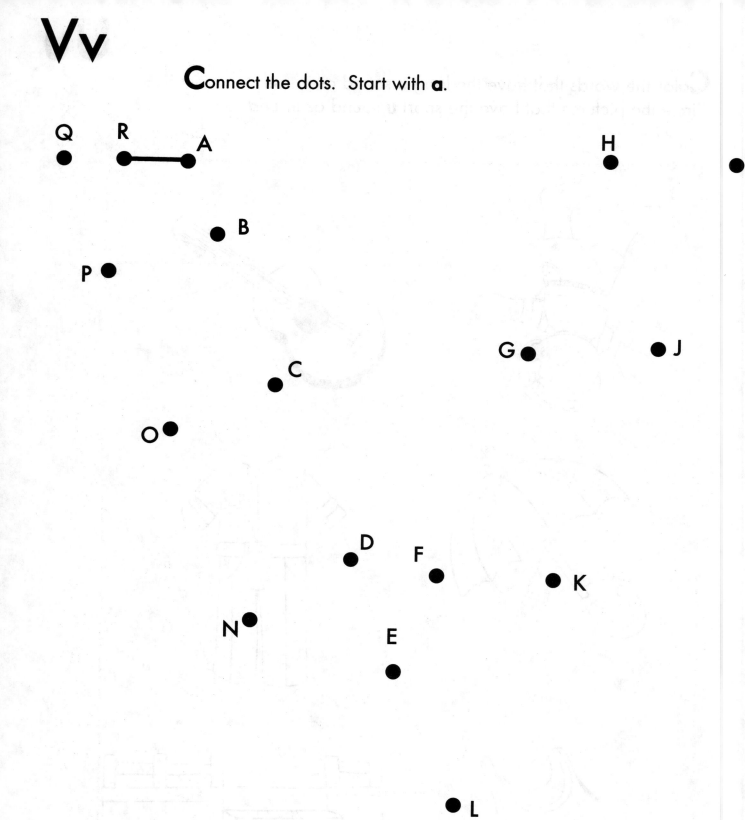

Q R A   H   I

B

P

G J

C

O

D F

K

N

E

L

M

Color all the spaces with **v** inside.

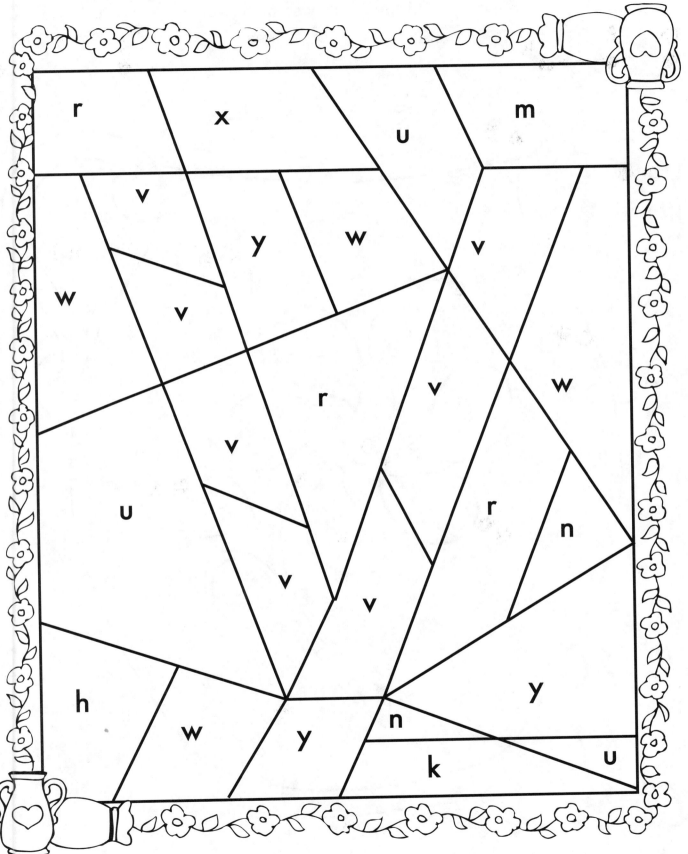

V is for *vase*. Color the vase. Cut it out.
Paste it on your paper. Draw some flowers in the vase.

108

V is for *vegetables*. Color the peas and lettuce green.
Color the carrots orange. Color the tomatoes red.
Color the beets purple.

Vv

V is for *valentine*. Color this valentine. Cut it out. Paste it on another piece of paper to give to someone special.

110

Connect the dots. Start with number 1.

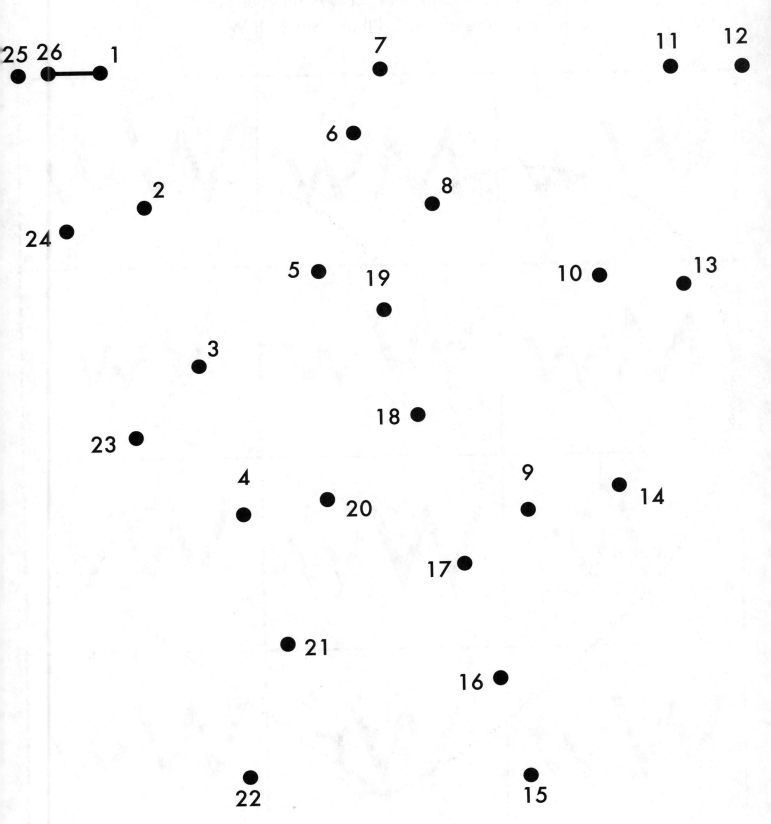

 **Ww**

Cut out the letter boxes.
Paste only the boxes with two **W**s on your paper.
Draw a picture of a word that starts with **W**.

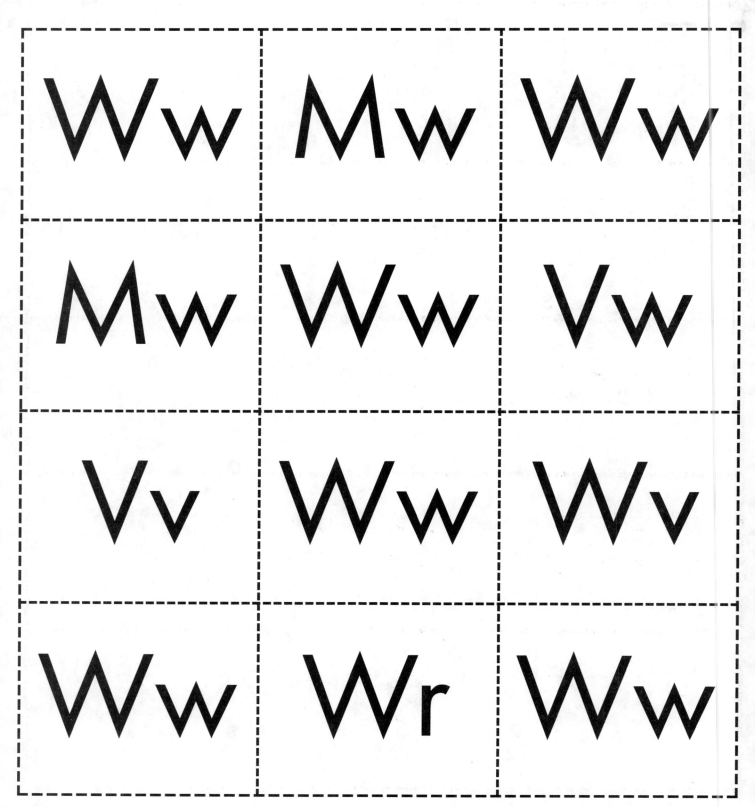

W is for *watermelon*. In each row, color the watermelon slice that has the *most* seeds.

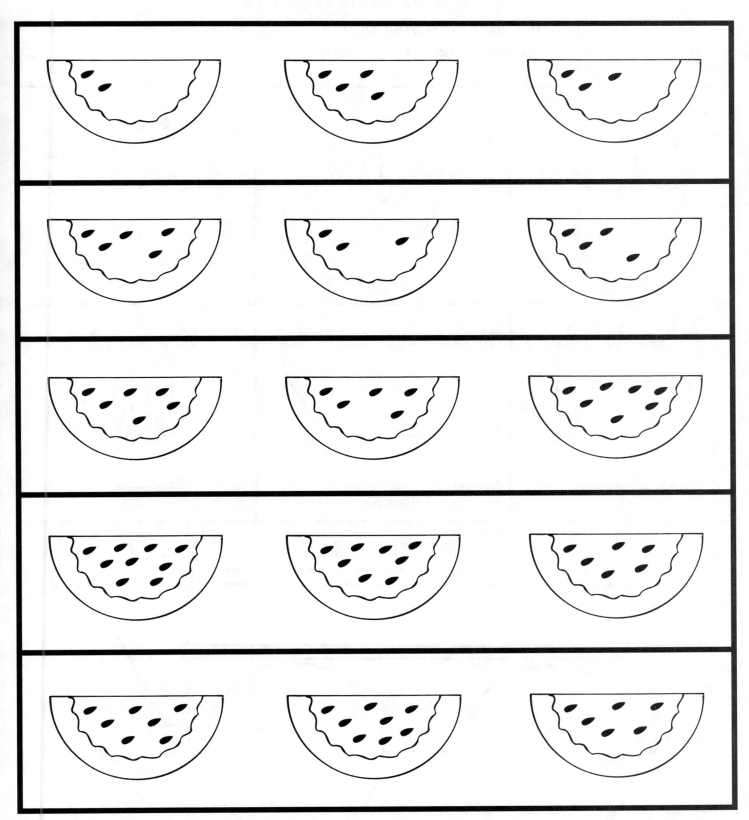

Ww

W is for *wagon*. Color the wagon.
Color the other pictures that start with **W**.
Cut out the wagon and all the **W** pictures.
Paste the wagon on your paper.
Paste the **W** pictures in the wagon.

whistle

wheel

frog

walrus

banana

wig

TLC10030 Copyright © Teaching & Learning Company, Carthage, IL 62321

W is for *waiter*. This waiter is serving your favorite meal.
Draw it on the waiter's tray and color the picture.

115

Xx

Trace and color.

116

TLC10030 Copyright © Teaching & Learning Company, Carthage, IL 62321

Connect the dots. Start with letter **A**.

V   W   A   E   F

B   G

U   D

C   H

T

S   I

N

J

R

O

M

Q   P   L   K

X is for *X-ray*. Cut out the pieces of the X-ray picture. Paste them on your paper to make a skeleton.

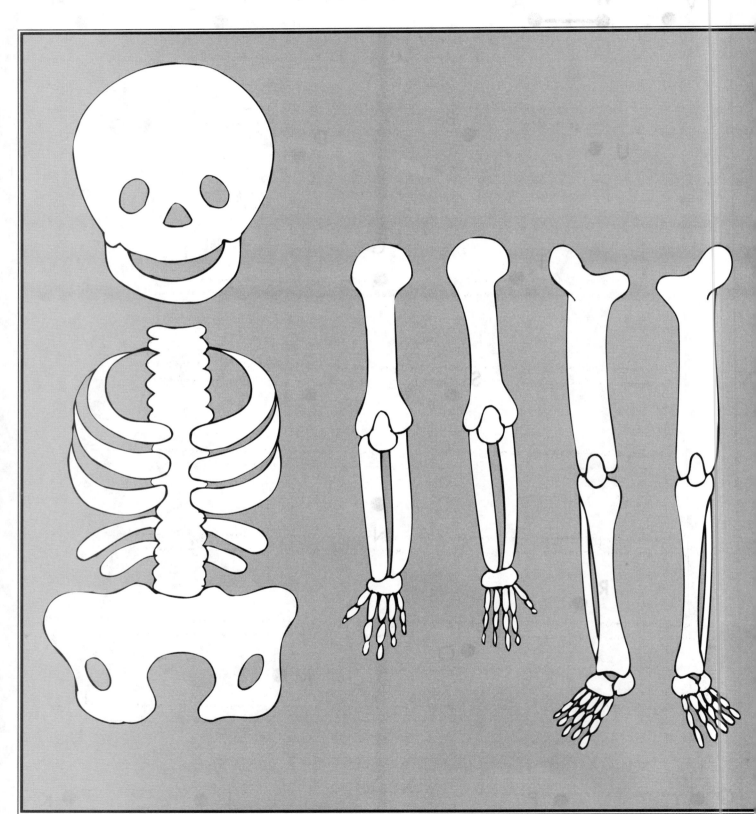

X is for *xylophone*. Color the bars of the xylophone in a pattern.

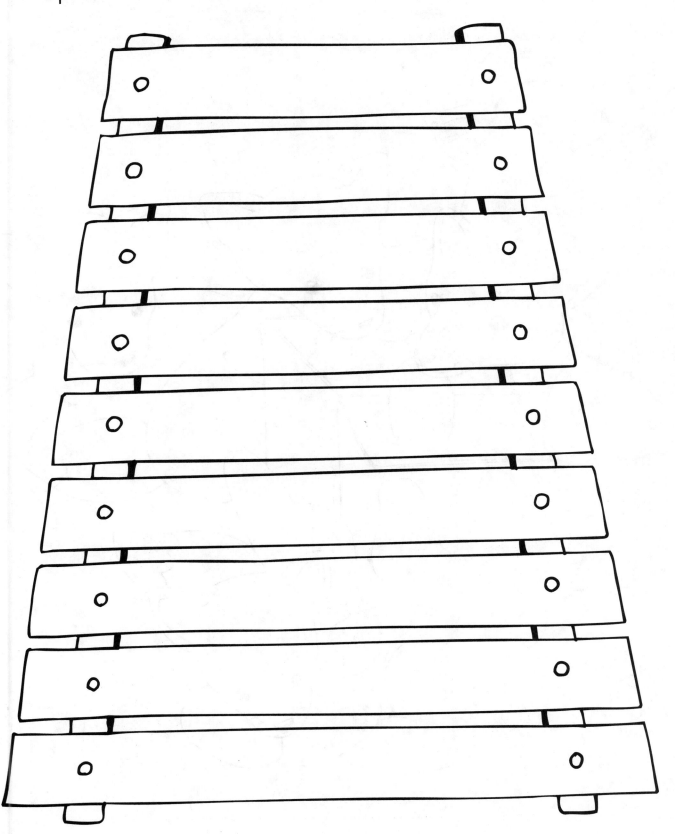

Xx

X is the last letter in *fox, box* and *six*. How many foxes do you see? Color them.

Color all the spaces with **Y** inside.

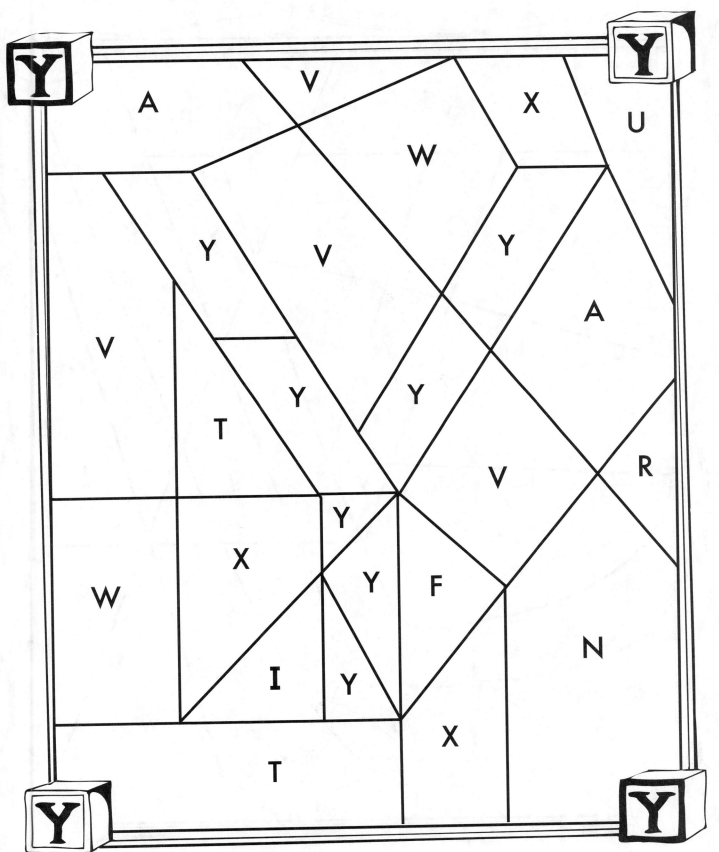

Yy

Color all the spaces with **y** inside.

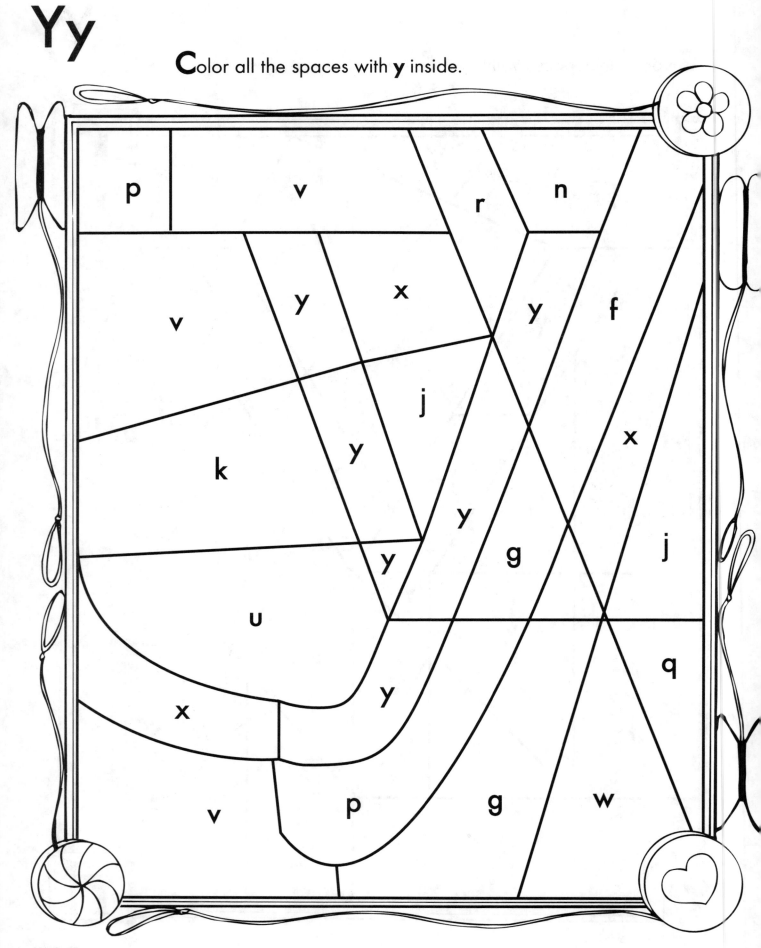

Y is for *yo-yo*. Trace each yo-yo to the right person.
Color the girl's yo-yo red.
Color the boy's yo-yo green.
Color the baby's yo-yo orange.
Color the man's yo-yo blue.
Color the picture.

Yy

Y is for *yard*. Color the yard. Color the swing, sandbox and slide. Cut them out. Paste them in the yard.

Yy

Y is for *yacht*. Color each circle on the yacht yellow. Color each square green. Color the water blue.

Zz

Connect the dots. Start at number 1.

1

21

20

19

2

3

4

18

5

17

6

16

7

15

8

9

10

14

13

12

11

Trace and color.

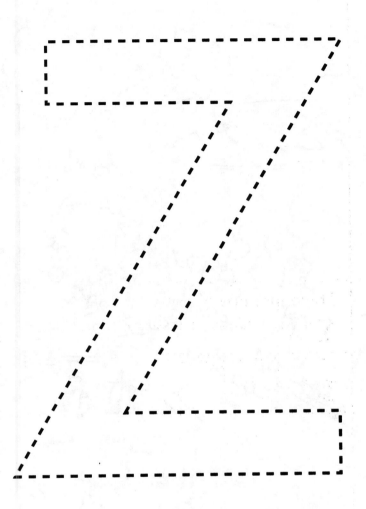

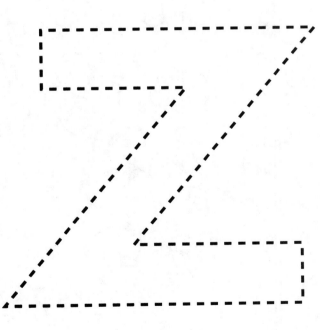

Zz

Z is for *zoo* and *zebra*. Help Zach go through the zoo and find the zebra. Color the picture.

Z is for *zigzag*. Color the zigzags. Cut them out. Paste them end to end on a long piece of paper.*

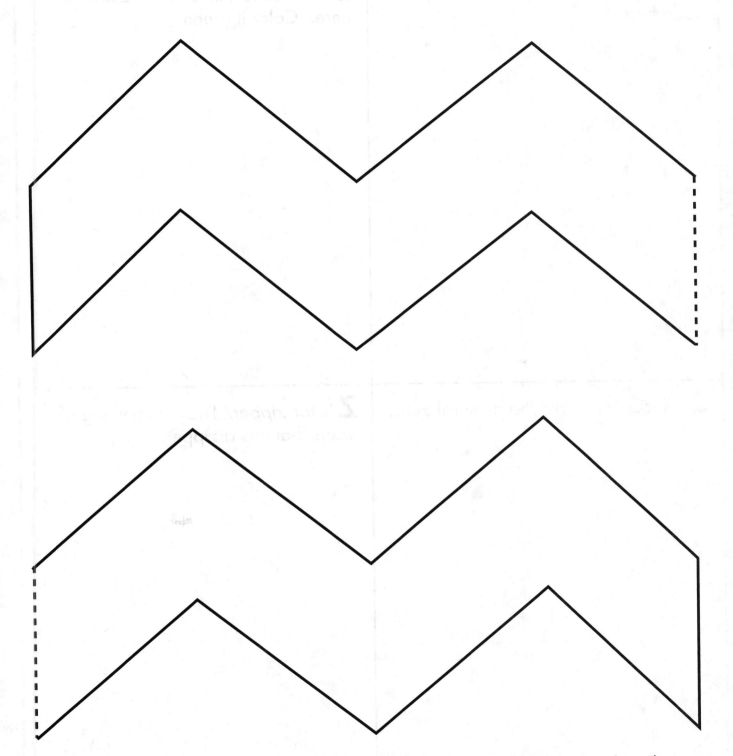

*Teacher: You may choose to make a classroom zigzag by connecting all of these on a long classroom wall.

Zz

Z is for *ZIP Code.* Write your zip code here.

Z is for *zucchini.* Draw a zucchini here. Color it green.

Z is for *zero.* Write the numeral zero.

Z is for *zipper.* Draw something of yours that has a zipper.

130

One shape in each row is written wrong. It could be backwards or mixed up in some way. Circle the incorrect letter in each row.

A	ᗺ	C	D	E	F
G	H	I	ᒧ	K	L
M	И	O	P	Q	R	S
T	U	V	W	X	Y	Z
ɒ	b	c	d	e	f	g
h	i	j	ĸ	l	m
n	o	p	q	r	ƨ
t	u	v	w	x	λ	z

A-Z

Cut out the capital letters at the right of the page.
Paste them in the correct spaces on the chart.

A	B	C	
E		G	H
I	J		L
M		O	P
Q	R	S	
U	V		X
Y	Z		

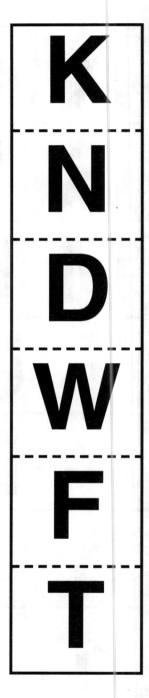

A-Z

Cut out the lowercase letters at the right of the page.
Paste them in the correct spaces on the chart.

a		c	d
e	f		h
i	j	k	
m	n		p
q		s	t
u	v	w	x
	z		

A-Z

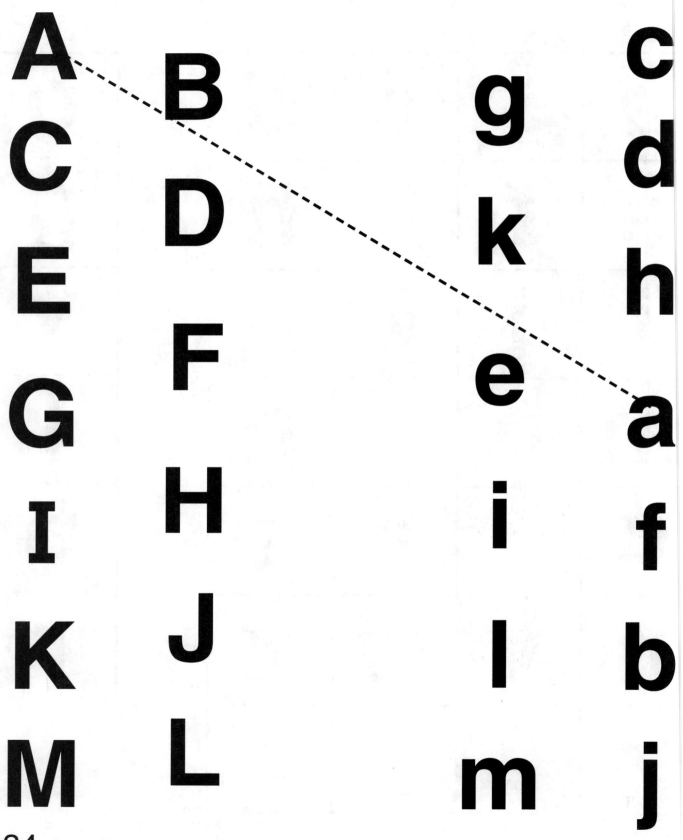

Draw a line to connect the capital letter to its lowercase letter.

A B c

g

C d

D

E k

F h

G e a

H

I i f

K

J

L b

M m j

134

TLC10030 Copyright © Teaching & Learning Company, Carthage, IL 62321

Draw a line to connect the capital letter to its lowercase letter.

N   O   n   p

P   t

R   Q   v   x

T   S   r   u

V   U   z   q

X   W   o   w

Z   Y   s   y

A-Z

In each box below, two letters of the alphabet are missing. When you know what they are, write those two letters in the empty spaces.

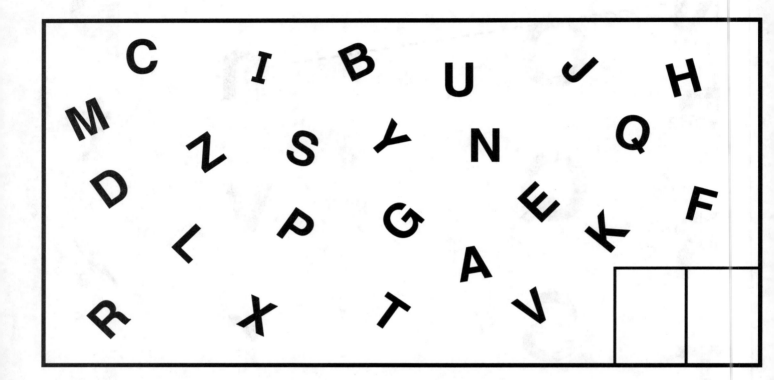

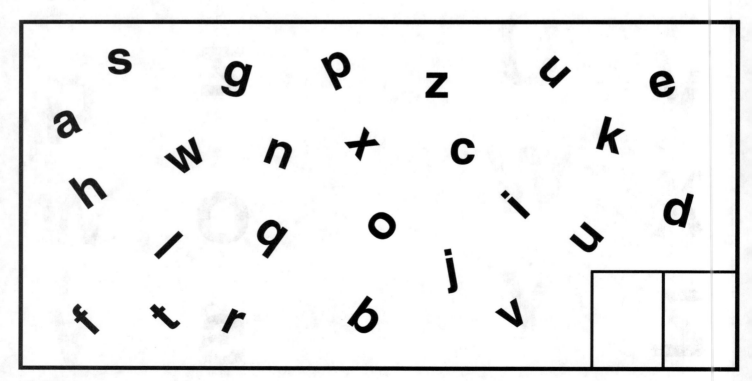

Answer Key

Page 5

Long **a**: ape, apron, anchor, angel
Short **a**: ant, ax, alligator, astronaut, antlers

Page 8

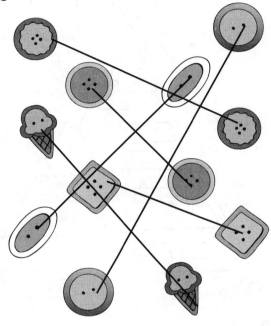

Page 9

These items should be circled:
baby butterfly, bird, boy

Page 13

Top picture: 10 circles
Bottom picture: 12 circles

Page 14

These words should be circled:
cent, celery, city, centipede

These words should be underlined:
cat, cake, coat, candy, cup

Page 19

Color the doll, duck, drum, dog.

Page 25

Long **e**: easel, Easter basket
Short **e**: Eskimo, envelope, elevator, elf

Page 29

These items should be circled in the bottom picture: cow, sun, window in roof, window in side of barn is gone, chick, no bush, hayloft door is different.

Page 34

Finished puzzles make a giraffe, goat and grasshopper.

Page 40

Circle the lion, book, truck, hammer.

Page 43

Answer Key

Page 44

Page 45

Long **i**: icicle, island, iron, iris
Long **i**: insect, inchworm

Page 54

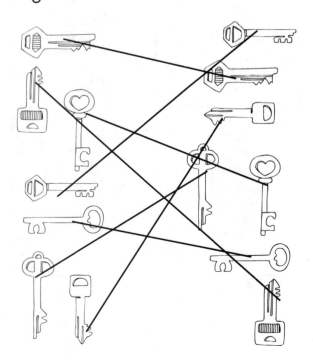

Page 58

These items should be colored: lamp, flashlight, candle, sun, lantern, light bulb.

Page 64

Page 65

The middle monkey has the most bananas.

Page 70

A	B	E	F
F	G	J	K
M	N	B	C
I	J	G	H
C	D	N	O
H	I	K	L
L	M	D	E

Answer Key

Page 73

Top picture: 9 ovals
Bottom picture: 10 ovals

Page 75

Long **o**: oval, oboe, oatmeal
Short **o**: olive, octopus, otter

Page 79

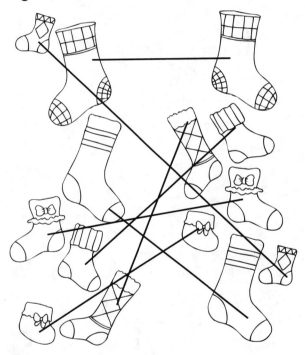

Page 85

Page 89

These reptiles should be colored:
snake, turtle, alligator.

Page 93

These animals should be colored:
seal, snake, skunk, sheep, snail, spider.

Page 94

These things should be circled in the
bottom picture: sailboat, cloud is missing, two birds are missing, one fish is
missing, one more starfish, one shell is
missing, seaweed on left is missing,
seaweed around sea horse is different.

Answer Key

Page 104

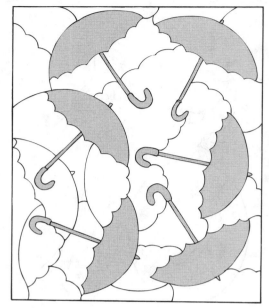

Page 105

Long **u**: ukulele, uniform
Short **u**: upside down, umbrella,
           undershirt, upstairs

Page 113

Row 1: Color the second slice.
Row 2: Color the first slice.
Row 3: Color the third slice.
Row 4: Color the first slice.
Row 5: Color the second slice.

Page 128

Page 131

A	B	C	D	E	F
G	H	I	J	K	L
M	N	O	P	Q	R	S
T	U	V	W	X	Y	Z
a	b	c	d	e	f	g
h	i	j	k	l	m
n	o	p	q	r	s
t	u	v	w	x	y	z

Page 136

Top box: The missing letters are **O** and **W**.
Bottom box: The missing letters are **m** and **y**.

140